Sophocles

The Theban Saga

IMMORTALS OF LITERATURE

Sophocles

FRANKLIN WATTS, INC.

Edited with an Introduction by

CHARLES ALEXANDER ROBINSON, JR.

The Theban Saga

575 LEXINGTON AVENUE, NEW YORK, N. Y. 10022

Acknowledgment is due the Yale University Press for its kind permission to reprint Clarence W. Mendell's translation of Sophocles' *Oedipus the King*, which first appeared in his *Our Seneca* (New Haven, 1941) and for which it holds the copyright.

For Celia Sachs Robinson

in admiration

Contents

Sophocles

The Theban Saga

Introduction

Perhaps more than any other Athenian, Sophocles typified the ancient Greek ideal that a man, no matter what his other ambitions and accomplishments, should live fully in the present. Sophocles has won immortality, to be sure, as the most human of Greek tragic poets, but during his long life he busied himself with many different activities. His birth in the fashionable Athenian suburb of Colonus and the advantages of wealth and education prepared him superbly for his varied career. In the year before he produced the *Antigone*, for instance, he was chosen by Pericles to be the chief treasurer of the Athenian empire, and two years later he was general in a war against the Aegean island of Samos.

Because Sophocles served the state in various capacities and mingled with all classes of people, it seems almost inevitable that this great artist should have concerned himself primarily with the human fortunes of his characters, with the effect of life upon a man's development and soul. The English essayist and poet Matthew Arnold summed it up rather exactly when he described Sophocles as the supreme example of a tragic poet "who saw life steadily and saw it whole."

Sophocles: The Theban Saga

A galaxy of brilliant men gathered in Athens during the Periclean Age—roughly, the second half of the glorious fifth century before Christ, 460–400 B.C. Some, like Sophocles, were dramatists; others were poets, historians, and philosophers; while still others were artists and architects who set up statues and buildings—the Parthenon among them—on the Athenian Acropolis. This was the time when Pericles brought his native Athens to a summit of civilization never before reached by the human race and seldom equaled since.

The closest link we have with the ancient Greeks is a common and passionate love of truth. Their devotion to clear and rational thought persuaded the best minds, at any rate, to place man in the center of things and to create the ideal of the dignity of the individual. This led, almost as a natural corollary, to the establishment of free democracy as a political institution, the first in the history of Europe. The tragic poets played a major role in introducing these advanced ideas to a large audience.

Greek tragic drama, whose origins lay in a dim and primitive past, was always associated with religion, no less than with human values and the responsibility of the individual. Aeschylus (c. 525–456 B.C.), the earliest of the three great Athenian tragedians, told his listeners that man, with the aid of the merciful gods, may work out his own redemption in suffering. Sophocles (c. 496–406 B.C.), on the other hand, did not regard himself as a teacher and merely presented the better side of the gods as normal; the gods appear in his plays to remind us that man, though free, does not live unto himself alone. Nor was Sophocles a skeptic, like his younger contemporary Euripides (c. 480–406 B.C.), who stood for individualism and insisted, as had the philosopher Protagoras, that "man is the measure of all things."

Sophocles went back to the imagined beginnings of the Greeks to find legends which might serve as the vehicles for

2

his dramas, but he so handled the myths that his plays reach the level of universal tragedy, ageless and altogether contemporary. He wrote over one hundred tragedies, but only seven survive entire. Three of these, though composed at different times, form a unit, and are known as the Theban Saga, for they deal with the House of Cadmus, the reputed founder of Thebes.

The House of Cadmus, because it had offended the gods, was doomed to be overwhelmed by catastrophe, especially in the person of Oedipus, its heir. Oedipus, completely ignorant of what he was doing, fulfilled the dread prophecy that he would slay his father and marry his mother; his children inherited the curse, for his sons killed each other in a civil war known to legend as "The Seven Against Thebes," and his daughter, Antigone, was buried alive. The extinction of the entire family is the story of the Theban Saga, as presented by Sophocles in *Oedipus the King, Oedipus at Colonus,* and *Antigone.*

Aristotle—the philosopher who lived a century later than Sophocles—took this general theme for his definition of tragedy. Tragedy, he says in his *Poetics,* should be a serious and complete "imitation" of an important action; it should arouse pity and fear and provide a catharsis, or purging, of these emotions. Ideally, Aristotle continues, the tragic hero should be a renowned man whose misfortune is brought upon him not by vice, but by frailty or an error of judgment. *Oedipus the King* illustrates this point nicely. Feelings of pity and fear are stirred by the tragic situation in which Oedipus finds himself, but by the end of the play Oedipus' noble conduct has purified these emotions in the minds of the audience.

As *Oedipus the King* unfolds, we learn that as soon as Oedipus was born, his parents, Laius and Jocasta, had ordered a slave to take the child to nearby Mount Cithaeron and there leave him to die. But the attractive baby had been rescued by a shepherd, who brought him back to Corinth. There the king and queen, Polybus and Merope, who wanted an heir, had reared the child as their son. Years later, during a drinking party, Oedipus was told that he was not the real son of Polybus and Merope. Terribly anxious to learn the truth about his birth, Oedipus sailed across the Corinthian Gulf to Delphi, where the oracle of the Pythian Apollo told him that he was destined to kill his father and marry his mother.

Without stopping to think the matter through—assuming, that is to say, that the king and queen of Corinth were his parents—Oedipus immediately set off in an easterly direction. At a lonely spot, where three roads came together, he met a haughty man who was riding to Delphi with his servants. The man was his real father, Laius, but neither father nor son knew the identity of the other. Both were short-tempered; they fell to fighting and then to quarreling, and the younger killed the older.

Oedipus continued his journey to Thebes, where a plague had fallen on the city. The plague would not be lifted, so it was said, until somebody guessed the riddle of the Sphinx, a monster who crouched by the road. "What creature is it," the Sphinx asked, "that walks on four legs in the morning, two at midday, and three in the evening?" Oedipus answered: "Man" (for late in life a man is likely to use a cane). At that, the Sphinx hurled herself to her death, the plague ended, and the grateful Thebans made Oedipus their king. Life does indeed often work out in a curious fashion; it seemed perfectly natural for Oedipus to marry Jocasta, the widow of the late king, thus fulfilling the oracle's prophecy that he would kill his father and marry his mother.

The years passed, Oedipus and Jocasta had children, and then suddenly another plague fell on the city. It is at this point that the first play in the Theban Saga opens. The reader or the audience may be overwhelmed by the tragedy of a man who was in the grip of forces greater than himself, but Oedipus, as he slowly learned the horrible truth, accepted the responsibility for his actions and offered no plea of ignorance.

The story is continued in *Oedipus at Colonus*. This is the last play by Sophocles, written when he was almost ninety and produced posthumously. A tragedy of great poetic beauty and power, it presents the final hours and death of Oedipus. Despite a certain mellowing of his nature with the passage of years, Oedipus still possesses the passionate spirit of his youth. He is an aged figure of heroic grandeur, innocent of an offense committed in ignorance and long since purified by his suffering. From the religious point of view the death of Oedipus represents the highest achievement of paganism. The ode in praise of Attica—the district in which Athens was located and in which Sophocles was born—glistening bright Colonus, with its nightingales and ivy, its myriad fruits and gentle dews of heaven—is one of the most beautiful ever written.

The *Antigone* concludes the Theban Saga, although it was the first of the three plays to be written. Two sons of Oedipus have fallen in single combat before Thebes—one of them a patriot, the other a rebel. Creon, the king, coldly orders that only the loyal brother may be buried, but Antigone, their sister, cannot make this distinction. Thus the play raises the eternal question of the relation between man's law and God's. A logical position, the play tells us, is often wrong; instinct and tradition can be right, for there is something higher than man-made law.

THE GREEK THEATER

Greek tragedies were first produced in the theater of Dionysus on the southern slope of the Athenian Acropolis during the *Dionysia,* a springtime festival in honor of Dionysus, patron saint of the theater and god of fertility. The whole production was in the hands of the author. Over a period of three successive days he presented a series of three plays which usually, though not always, dealt with the same theme. Only one such trilogy, the *Oresteia* of Aeschylus, has survived from antiquity.

Since Dionysus was worshiped as a god, a religious atmosphere surrounded these productions. The days on which the tragedies were presented were long and serious. The audience was the most critical in history because its members

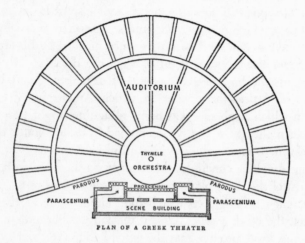

PLAN OF A GREEK THEATER

were not only well acquainted with the great dramas of the past and the present, but it also numbered many who had already taken part in dramatic exhibitions. The presentations were keenly competitive, as was much of Greek life (witness the Olympic Games). A committee selected the playwrights who were to be allowed to produce their dramas, and at the end of the performances they pronounced their verdicts and awarded prizes to the best players and actors.

As a rule, there were three actors in a Greek tragedy, though an actor might be called upon to take more than one part. These actors were always men. Since the theater was so large that it was impossible for the audience to catch changes in facial expression, the actors wore masks to show what kind of characters they portrayed. The masks also had the additional value of serving as megaphones, although ancient theaters are famous for their good acoustics.

In addition to its three actors, a Greek tragedy also had a chorus made up of fifteen amateurs, for whose training a wealthy citizen was assigned to pay. In the beginning, the chorus had a role almost equivalent to that of an actor, but in time its importance decreased. It had a way, however, of making the audience feel itself a part of the play, because it often reflected public opinion. Occasionally it was able to glimpse the future, too. As the chorus sang and went through certain evolutions, a pair of choral passages came to be known as *strophe* and *antistrophe* (turn and counterturn). We know that singing and dancing were integral parts of Greek drama, though the details have been lost.

The theater of Dionysus at Athens was open to the sky and seated approximately 18,000 persons. Below the stone seats of the auditorium was a level circular area, known as the orchestra. Chorus and actors performed there. In the middle of the orchestra was the *thymelē*, an altar to Dionysus; beside it sat the musicians. Behind the orchestra stood a long structure for the storage of costumes and other properties, known as the scene building (in Greek, *skēnē*—"tent"—from which comes our word *scene*); the actors made their entrances from the *skēnē*. In front of the structure, and almost tangent with the orchestra, was a line of columns called the *proscenium*, which served as a background for actors and chorus. Painted panels were usually set between the columns to serve as scenery, which was very simple, as it was in Shakespeare's day. There was a projection forward (called the *parascenium*) at either end of the proscenium; between parascenium and orchestra was the entrance passage (*parodos*) for chorus and audience.

In recent years there has been an upsurge of interest in

7

Greek drama. The ancient plays have been performed with increasing frequency by both amateur and professional groups. Their influence is clear in the work of many playwrights who try to explain man's frustration and feeling of isolation in an expanding mechanized society. How has man failed, they appear to ask, that he should be cursed by the gods with fear of the thing he has created in innocence? The modern writer has not in most instances, however, been able to produce the true heroic character who, through suffering and by his own strength and courage and realization of personal dignity, purges himself and his audience of sin.

Charles Alexander Robinson, Jr.

SOPHOCLES

❖❖❖❖❖❖❖❖❖

Oedipus the King

Translated by Clarence W. Mendell

CHARACTERS IN THE PLAY

OEDIPUS, *king of Thebes*

PRIEST OF ZEUS

JOCASTA, *queen of Thebes; widow of Laius, the late king, and now wife of Oedipus*

CREON, *brother of Jocasta*

TEIRESIAS, *a blind prophet*

A MESSENGER, *from Corinth*

A HERDSMAN, *formerly in the service of Laius*

SECOND MESSENGER

CHORUS *of Theban Elders*

CROWD OF SUPPLIANTS, *men, women, and children*

ARGUMENT

Laius and Jocasta, king and queen of Thebes, had received a warning from an oracle that a son born to them would kill his father and marry his mother. When the son was born, he was brought to Mount Cithaeron, rescued, and reared as the son of Polybus and Merope, king and queen of Corinth. Some years later, when a strange monster, known as the Sphinx, began to kill the people of Thebes, Laius went to Delphi to seek the oracle's aid. On the way, he was slain. Not long afterward, Oedipus came to Thebes. He guessed the Sphinx's riddle. The grateful Thebans offered him the throne and the hand of Jocasta. Several years pass, and two sons and two daughters are born to Oedipus and Jocasta. The play opens at a point when pestilence has fallen on Thebes. Though Oedipus offers no plea of ignorance as he learns the horrible truth about himself, but accepts the responsibility for his acts, are we not overwhelmed nevertheless by the tragedy of man powerless in the face of forces greater than himself?

Before the palace of Oedipus at Thebes. Nearby is an altar, beside which stand a priest and suppliants of all ages. Oedipus enters.

OEDIPUS: My children, ancient Cadmus' newest brood,
            What is this embassy that waits impatient,
            Bedecked with suppliant branches? All our town
            Is filled with sound of holy sacrifice,
            And paeans, too, and wailing misery.
            These things, my children, I have deemed it wrong
            To learn from others: I went forth myself,
            I, famed on the lips of all men, Oedipus.
            But tell me, sire—for thou art fit to speak
            For these—in what mood stand ye there? In fear
            Or loyalty? Stony of heart the man
            Who finds no pity for such embassy.

PRIEST: O Oedipus, that rulest o'er my land,
            Thou seest us, how of every age we sit
            Before thy altars, some not yet endowed
            With strength for distant flight, and some
            Heavy with age who serve as priests (myself
            The priest of Zeus), and other some elect
            From all the tribes. Within the market-place
            Sits the whole populace in suppliant garb
            By Pallas' twofold shrine revered, or where
            Ismenus' sacred soil speaks prophecy.
            For, as thou seest too, our commonwealth
            Labors full sore nor yet avails to lift
            Its head above the billowing surge of death,
            Wasting alike in the rich crops of earth

And in her grazing herds, while women suffer
The pangs of barren childbirth. Through her midst
The fire-bearing god, mad pestilence,
Hurling his shafts, scourges relentlessly
Our city till, beneath his hand, the home
Of Cadmus is made void, and Hades black
With groans and lamentations is enriched.
Not with the gods do I now make thee one,
Nor these thy children seated at thy gate,
But first of all mankind we reckon thee
In ways of men and in perplexities
Haling from heaven above. 'Twas thou that camest,
Loosing our Cadmeian city from the toll
We paid the singer of harsh harmonies,
Learning no clue from us: no other man
Instructed thee but by the lore of god,
Men say, believing, thou didst right our life.
Now too, O Oedipus, that rulest all,
Turning to thee we all petition thee:
Discover straight some remedy for us.
It may be thou shalt hearken to the voice
Of god or of some man, thou knowest whose.
For yesterday's experience methinks
Best validates the counsel of today.
Up then, and save thy city, thou who art
Best of mankind; up, gird thyself, for thee
This country calls its savior, honoring
Thy past devotion. Never let memory
Recall thy rule, how once erect we stood
Upraised only to fall. Nay, save the state.
A happy rescue from the cursed Sphinx
Thou gavest us long since: be now the same.
And thou wouldst rule this city as thou dost,
Better to rule o'er men than emptiness.

Fortress and ship alike become as naught
Bereft of humankind to dwell therein.

OEDIPUS: My children pitiable, not strange to me,
Familiar rather are the things ye ask.
Full well I know your anguish—yet, howe'er
Ye suffer all, there is no one of you
Whose suffering equals mine. Your several griefs
Touch each one man, no other than yourselves:
My spirit groans for all the city—ay,
For me and you alike. Ye rouse me not
From sleep, for, be assured, I have shed tears
Uncounted; many a path my mind has traced,
And that which I have found—one only means
To remedy our lot—that have I followed,
Sending Menoeceus' son, my brother Creon,
Unto Apollo's Pythian shrine to learn
What word or act of mine might save the state.
Already with the loitering length of days
Time tortures me in wonder how he fares.
For well beyond what old experience
Bids us expect he still is absent. When
He comes, I shall not then be derelict
In my fulfilment of god's whole behest.

PRIEST: Timely thy word, O King, for these but now
Point me to where already Creon comes.

OEDIPUS: O Lord Apollo, may he come endued
With bright good fortune, as his eye is bright.

PRIEST: 'Tis safe to hazard that his news is good:
Else not with fruited laurel were he decked.

OEDIPUS: Soon shall we know for he can hear us now.
My lord and kinsman, son of Menoeceus,
What message dost thou bring us from the god?

(Enter Creon.)

CREON: Good news, for I declare that even ills,
If they but end aright, may all be well.

OEDIPUS: What news is this? For neither bold of heart
Nor fearful am I at thy present word.

CREON: If thou wouldst hear in presence of these men
I am prepared to speak—or else within.

OEDIPUS: Speak to them all. Heavier the grief I bear
For them than for my own heart's suffering.

CREON: Speak then I will my message from the god.
Lord Phoebus bade us all outspokenly
Drive forth the pestilence that's bred within
Our land nor fatten it beyond control.

OEDIPUS: And with what exorcism? What is the means?

CREON: Exile or death, repaying ancient death.
For blood it is that overwhelms our state.

OEDIPUS: Upon what man does god decree this chance?

CREON: Laius, my lord, was one time sovereign here
Over our land, ere ever thou didst come.

OEDIPUS: I know by hearsay, for I saw him not.

CREON: And he being dead, comes clear god's high command
Forthwith to punish those his murderers.

OEDIPUS: And they are where? Where shall be found the clue
Hard to unravel of such ancient crime?

CREON: Within this land he said. That which is sought
Is found; the unconsidered vanishes.

OEDIPUS: At home or in the country or abroad

Did Laius happen on his bloody fate?

CREON: Faring upon a mission, as he said,
Laius returned no more from his emprise.

OEDIPUS: No comrade of the road, no messenger
Beheld the deed that one might learn from him?

CREON: Dead are they all save one who terrified
Fled with one word alone of all he saw.

OEDIPUS: And what was that? One thing may lead to much
If we but gain some slight foothold of hope.

CREON: Robbers, he said, encountered on the way,
Not one but many, killed him ruthlessly.

OEDIPUS: How could a robber save by gold suborned
From Thebes, attain to such bold arrogance?

CREON: Suspicion spake as much but, Laius dead,
No champion was there in our misery.

OEDIPUS: What dread disaster could restrain the state
From learning all, its master so destroyed?

CREON: The riddling Sphinx compelled us to resign
Mystery remote for questions close at hand.

OEDIPUS: From the beginning then I'll prove it clear.
For just is Phoebus, rightly too thyself
Hast laid on me this duty to the dead.
So shalt thou find me rightly an ally
Unto this land obedient to the god.
For not alone as boon to distant friends
But for myself I'll scotch this pestilence.
Seeing that whoso slew him, he likewise
Fearing my venging hand, might slay me too.
Hence if I fail him not I benefit
Myself. Up then, my people, speedily

Stand from these altars, raise your suppliant staves.
Let someone gather here the citizens
Of Thebes, assured that I shall compass all
And we shall stand revealed all fortunate
Under god's guiding help—or fallen quite.

PRIEST: My children, let us rise. It was for this
Which now he tells us that we gathered here,
And so may Phoebus with his oracle
Be savior too and end the pestilence.

(*Exeunt. Enter Chorus of Theban Elders.*)

Strophe 1

CHORUS: O thou Word sweet spoken, of Zeus
                        How shall I name thee?
              Forth from the Pythian shrine
              Gleaming with gold art come
                        Unto glorious Thebes.
And my quivering heart is taut and I shudder with fear,
                        Thou Delian God,
                   As low on my knees I pray.
              Comes there a fate unknown
              Or again with the circling years
                        Recurring woe?
Tell me, thou child of golden Hope, Word ever living.

Antistrophe 1

              First to thee, O daughter of Zeus,
                   Deathless Athena,
              Make I my suppliant prayer;
              Artemis too I call
                        She who ranges the hills

And she sits on the throne high raised in the gathering
   place;
            And Phoebus who shoots
        Afar over earth his darts:
        Threefold defenders, come
        As of old at our city's need
           Ye came to save,
Banishing far the flame of woe: come now to save us.

Strophe 2

Woe, woe is me, countless the pains I bear;
        All that is mine is doomed:
           No shaft of wit
        Brings me deliverance;
        No generations new
        To cherish my fatherland.
No more do the mothers of Thebes, bearing their sons,
        Suffer the pain and live,
But soul on soul, like birds, ye may see them fly
           Swifter than fire
On to the distant strand, home of the western god.

Antistrophe 2

Beyond our ken, countless the city's dead;
        Foul on the plain they lie
           In cruel ranks;
        Mothers bereft, gray haired,
        In supplication bent,
        And wives by the altar side,
They groan for the ills that are ours: sorrows untold:
        Paeans of woe that burst
From aged lips that moan for a city doomed.

Wherefore for these
Send us some bulwark fair, golden daughter of Zeus.

Strophe 3

Ares too, god of the raging death:
Helmet nor shield are his
But the flame and the shouting.
Back, turn him back, far from our fatherland,
Back on a favoring breeze
To Amphitrite's couch
Or the harbor welcomeless of the Thracian surge.
For now if the night leave aught
Day comes apace to consume.
O, father above, on him,
Lord of the lightning flash,
Hurl now thy thunderbolt.

Antistrophe 3

Lord of light, god of the golden bow
Scatter thy shafts untamed
To defend us, we pray thee.
Aye and the fire gleaming of Artemis
Which on the Lycian hills,
She flashes peak by peak;
And the golden mitered god of our native land
Whose face with the wine is red,
Bacchus, I call, with thy rout
Of maenads attended, come.
Come with the flaming torch,
Smite thou the god disowned.

(*Enter Oedipus.*)

OEDIPUS:

Ye pray, and what ye pray for—if straightway
Ye hearken to my words and give me aid
Against the pestilence—ye may attain:
Deliverance and surcease from your woes—
Words of a stranger to this history,
A stranger to the deed. Not far alone
Could I without a hint pursue the quest.
Wherefore, your latest citizen, do I
Make proclamation to the Cadmeian land:
Whoso of you knows by whose hand assailed
Laius the son of Labdacus was slain,
I bid him tell me all. But if he fear
For his own self, then let him none the less
Denounce himself, for he shall suffer naught
Save banishment. So too if any man
Knows that the culprit came from other lands,
Let him not hold his tongue, for whoso speaks
Reward is his and gratitude beside.
But if ye will not speak, if dumb with fear
Ye seek to shield or friend or self from harm,
Then hearken to the purpose that is mine.
No man soever from this sovereign realm
Whose rule is mine, by shelter or by word
Shall aid the murderer, or e'er admit
His presence at the litany or shrine
Of sacrifice or at the lustral fire,
But thrust him from his home, knowing full well
He is the accursed thing as now the god
By Pythian oracle hath made us know.
So do I purpose to ally myself
With god and with the dead. Here I invoke
This curse upon the guilty one or all
Wretched to plumb the depths of misery.
Likewise upon myself if knowingly

I harbor in my house the murderer
I imprecate the curses I have named.
So upon each of you I lay a charge
To heed these words—for my sake and the god's
And for our city in its barrenness
Abandoned of the gods and perishing.
For even if it were not sent from heaven,
This plague upon us, yet, 'twere unthinkable
To leave still unavenged the death
Of one so noble and your king withal,
Nor track it down. Now since I hold the power
That once was his, and am the heir as well
Of his own marriage couch, possess the wife
That lay with him and would have borne to us
A common offspring had not fate ill timed,
Striking him down, forbidden, I pronounce
Myself his champion, even as his son,
And I shall leave no single thing untried
To find and seize that man who put to death
The son of Labdacus, heir to the line
Of Polydorus and of Cadmus too,
Ancient Agenor's latest progeny.
Meantime for such as see not eye to eye
With this my purpose, I invoke the gods
To grant them harvest neither in their fields
Nor in their homes, but with this pestilence
Or some more terrible, to end their line.
But citizens of this Cadmeian realm
That hearken to my words, on them I pray
May Justice smile forever and the gods.

CHORUS: O King, upon my oath as thou dost ask
I speak: I did not kill the man, nor know
The murderer. To say who did the deed
Was Phoebus' task who laid on us the quest.

OEDIPUS: Right is thy judgment, but to force the gods
           Unwilling, that may no man undertake.

CHORUS: Fain would I say what seemeth second best.

OEDIPUS: If there be yet a third best, speak it out.

CHORUS: After lord Phoebus he who seeth most
           In harmony, our lord Teiresias,
           Might best reward our present questioning.

OEDIPUS: Nor has this thought escaped me. I have sent
           At Creon's bidding twice to summon him,
           Nor understand why he came not long since.

CHORUS: All other hints were vague and ancient tales.

OEDIPUS: What hints then are there? I would know each word.

CHORUS: 'Twas said some travelers had murdered him.

OEDIPUS: So have I heard, but none saw him who saw.

CHORUS: Nor if he knows what fear is will he stay
           When he has heard thy curses now invoked.

OEDIPUS: Words may not frighten him who fears no deed.

CHORUS: But lo he comes who shall convict the man.
           For these are bringing now the godlike seer
           In whom alone of men is born the truth.

           (Enter Teiresias, led by a boy.)

OEDIPUS: Teiresias, who mind doth ponder all
           Things known and things unspeakable on earth
           And in the heavens above, though seeing naught
           Thou knowest in what plight our city stands
           Wherefrom, my lord, we find in thee alone
           Our sole deliverer. For Phoebus' word

(Perchance thou hast not heard from messengers)
Comes back in answer to our questionings
Telling of one release from pestilence
And only one, if we by searching out
Should find and slay forthwith the murderers
Of Laius or should drive them from our land.
Wherefore begrudge us not thy counseling
Whether from augury or from the lore
Of other ways prophetic thou knowest aught.
But save alike thyself, the city, me,
And fend from all the taint of murder done.
For we are in thy hands: man's noblest toil
Is helping others to the uttermost.

TEIRESIAS: Alas, alas, how frightful to be wise
Where wisdom brings no gain. I knew this well
But had forgotten. Else had I never come.

OEDIPUS: What sayest thou? How downcast art arrived.

TEIRESIAS: Release me to my home. Most easily
Shall we two bear our fates, if thou consent.

OEDIPUS: Strange are thy words nor friendly to the state
That gives thee sustenance, if thou speak not.

TEIRESIAS: Not so: for thine own words as I perceive
Come not in season. Be not mine the same.

OEDIPUS: By all the gods I beg thee, leave us not,
If thou knowest aught, me and these suppliants.

TEIRESIAS: Aye for ye all are ignorant. Mine own
Misfortunes shall I hide, to speak not thine.

OEDIPUS: What is this word? Thou knowest and wilt not speak
But wouldst betray thy city unto death?

TEIRESIAS: Neither myself nor thee shall I distress.
Why ask in vain? Thou shalt not learn from me.

OEDIPUS: Basest of all base men, that wouldst enrage
The hardest rock, wilt never speak, but still
Present thyself unmoved in stubbornness?

TEIRESIAS: My wrath thou blamest but thine own so near
Thou seest not, and yet upbraidest me.

OEDIPUS: Who would not rage to hear such words as thine
Wherewith even now thou dost outrage the state?

TEIRESIAS: 'Twill come though by my silence hidden deep.

OEDIPUS: Then what will come thou too must speak to me.

TEIRESIAS: I'll speak no further; wherefore if thou wilt,
Vent to the full thy wildest storm of rage.

OEDIPUS: Truly I'll leave unsaid no single word
Of all I think. Such is my rage. Know then
What I believe: that thou didst plot this deed.
Performed it too save only that thy hands
Wrought not the act. And hadst thou now thy sight
I'd say the murder too was all thine own.

TEIRESIAS: Is't true? I charge thee then from thy decree
Swerve not, nor from this day forevermore
Speak unto these or me: thou art the man
That bringest on this land the curse of guilt.

OEDIPUS: Thus shameless wouldst thou speak and still expect
Somewhere to find a refuge from thy fate?

TEIRESIAS: Safety is mine. I speak the all powerful truth.

OEDIPUS: Who taught thee then? 'Twas not thy priestly art.

TEIRESIAS: I learned of thee, that forced my unwilling speech.

OEDIPUS: What speech? Lest I should err, speak it once more.

23

TEIRESIAS:	Hast thou not known or wouldst thou spread a net?
OEDIPUS:	Unknowable it seems—speak it again.
TEIRESIAS:	I say thou art the slayer that thou wouldst find.
OEDIPUS:	Not to thy joy hast spoken twice such words.
TEIRESIAS:	Shall I say more then that shall irk thee more?
OEDIPUS:	Say what thou wilt for thou shalt say in vain.
TEIRESIAS:	I say that thou hast lived most shamefully Unwitting with thy kin, nor knowest thy plight.
OEDIPUS:	Does think unharmed still to repeat such things?
TEIRESIAS:	Aye, if there be in truth protecting strength.
OEDIPUS:	There is, for all save thee—but not for thee For thou are blind in ear and mind and eye.
TEIRESIAS:	These jeerings prove thee wretched, for e'er long Each man of these shall hurl them back at thee.
OEDIPUS:	Thou dwellest in continuous night, nor canst Hurt me or any man that sees the day.
TEIRESIAS:	'Tis not thy fate to fall by hand of mine. Apollo shall suffice, the charge is his.
OEDIPUS:	Was't Creon's thought or thine this treachery?
TEIRESIAS:	Creon ne'er did thee harm but thou thyself.
OEDIPUS:	O Wealth and Power and Craft outreaching craft Throughout our jealous life. What envious thrust Can we be safe from if for this throne's sake Whereof by gift I ne'er solicited Thebes made me master, if for this my lord Creon the faithful, friend since first I came, Secretly plotting seeks to thrust me forth,

Suborning for his end this muddling priest
That knows the wiles of wealth, sees faultlessly
Where gain is for the getting, yet straightway
Sought for his priestcraft stumbles and is blind.
For tell me when hast thou shown prophecy?
Why when the riddling bitch bedeviled us
Didst thou not speak some safety to the state?
'Twas hardly for a chance arrival then
To spell that riddle, prophecy forsooth
Was needed then. Yet from thy twittering birds
Thou spakest naught, nor knewest aught from god.
'Twas I who came, I, Oedipus, that had
No knowledge of it all, and yet prevailed
By simple wisdom with no lore of birds.
Whom thou wouldst exile in the expectancy
Of high position close to Creon's throne.
Sorrow shall be the harvest—thine and his—
Of this prophetic sowing. Wert not old
Such thought as thine should bring thee violence.

CHORUS: Oedipus, both his words and thine appear
Spoken in anger, so at least I judge.
Such words we need not: be it our concern
How best we may fulfill god's oracle.

TEIRESIAS: Tyrant thou art—yet cannot so refuse
The right to answer. That much lies within
My power. No slave am I to thee or any man
Beside—only to Loxias. Wherefore
Write me not down to Creon's patronage.
Thou chidest me with blindness. Hear me say
That eyes thou hast but seest not thy plight,
Not even where thou livest nor with whom.
Dost know from whom thou'rt born? Nay, ignorant,
Thou hast made thyself the foe of thine own kin

25

That dwell with Hades or yet tread the earth.
Thee shall thy mother's curse, thy father's too,
Swift footed, two edged, drive from out this land
With eyes that see now, seeing then no more.
What refuge there that shall not echo back
Thy piteous cry—what haunt of desolate
Cithaeron—when thou seest the anchorage
Whither on favoring breeze, into this home
Thou hast sailed in to shipwreck. Other ills
Countless (thou seest them not) shall level thee
With thine own self and thy begotten seed.
Revile thou as thou wilt the word I speak
And Creon too, for in the whole wide world
No man shall be so smitten as thyself.

OEDIPUS: Can such things then be borne from such as he?
Begone to thy perdition—get thee gone—
Out of this house—begone I say, begone.

TEIRESIAS: I had not come hadst thou not summoned me.

OEDIPUS: I knew thee not, that thou wouldst speak the fool,
Or I had never brought thee to my house.

TEIRESIAS: I am but as I am—to thee a fool,
Yet wise indeed to those that gave thee birth.

OEDIPUS: Who? Stay. Canst say who 'twas that gave me birth?

TEIRESIAS: This day shall give thee birth and give thee death.

OEDIPUS: Forever riddles, riddles, dost thou speak.

TEIRESIAS: And art not thou the best to answer these?

OEDIPUS: Chide me with that. Thou'lt find me fortunate.

TEIRESIAS: That was the fortune that hath ruined thee.

OEDIPUS: I care not if the city so be saved.

TEIRESIAS: Then do I go—come boy and lead me home.

OEDIPUS: Aye, let him lead thee, lingering here thou art
A nuisance, 'twere relief to have thee gone.

TEIRESIAS: I go for I have spoken that for which
I came, nor feared thy face; thou hast no power
Over my lips. But hark to what I say.
He whom thou seekest issuing thy threats
And heralding the death of Laius—he
Dwells here within—an alien visitor—
So is the tale—but shall appear at last
Native-born Theban—yet no joy be his
At that discovery. For blind where once
He saw, a rich man beggared, he shall go
Forth to a foreign land feeling his way
With helpless staff, proving at last to be
Brother and sire to his own progeny.
And unto her that bore him in the womb
Both son and husband, to his aged sire
Betrayer first and then his murderer.
Go thou within and on these prophecies
Think well—if in one single circumstance
Thou find me false, denounce my prophet's role.

(Exeunt Teiresias and Oedipus separately.)

Strophe 1

CHORUS: Voice, god-sent from Delphi's rock,
Whose was the deed
Ill-wrought with blood-stained hands
Unspeakable? To lands
Afar with the speed wind-swift of the winged steed
Now must he take his flight nor longer mock

The embattled son of Zeus that leaps
> Swift following
With the brandished flame that never sleeps
And Fate insatiate unpitying.

Antistrophe 1

Flashing from Parnassus' peaks
> Gleaming with snow
> Behest imperative
> To find the fugitive
That far through the trackless wood and the caves below
> Wanders alone distraught and ever seeks
> To avert the doom whose heartless Fate
> Relentlessly
From Apollo's shrine immaculate
Pursuing shapes unmoved his destiny.

Strophe 2

Dread is the word, dread is the augury,
> And the truth who knows?
Words have I none: fluttering hopes I see
> And anon fear in their place. For the morrow shows
> Darkness deep as today.
> What old grief can I say
Breeding hate of our royal line
Now might sully the fame long won
> By Polybus' son
Or fasten on him the doom of the word divine.

Antistrophe 2

Zeus knoweth all, Zeus and the Delphian lord

With all-seeing eye.
Yea, but of man, priests with prophetic word
Why unto them yield we credulity?
Though in wisdom of mind
Man may humble mankind,
Never shall I till the truth be clear
Grant his guilt who released our state
From ruinous Fate
Outwitted the riddling monster and banished fear.

(*Enter Creon.*)

CREON: My fellow citizens, I am informed
That Oedipus the King hath uttered here
Grave charges against me. And so I come
Resentful, seeing that in our present plight
If he believe that aught in word or deed
From me hath injured him, I have no will
Under suspicion to prolong my life.
Not simple is the harm that such a charge
Does me but manifold if I am thought
False to my city and to you, my friends.

CHORUS: Such was the charge he made perchance
Not in cool wisdom but in bitter wrath.

CREON: And said he also that by my advice
The seer put forth his lying prophecies?

CHORUS: So spake he but with what intent, who knows?

CREON: But with a mind unclouded and clear eye
Brought he this charge against me? Tell me that.

CHORUS: I know not. For I am not wont to see
What kings perform. But look, he comes himself.

(*Enter Oedipus.*)

OEDIPUS: Thou? Thou? How art thou come? Such brazen front
Of daring hast thou as to approach my house,
The murderer proven of this man and now
Usurper manifest of this my throne?
Come tell me by the gods, was't cowardice
Or folly seen in me that tempted thee
To such a plotting or didst think the act
Would not betray thy stealthy treachery
Or even perchance that I might wittingly
Ignore it? Is it not a fool's attempt
With neither force nor friends to seek a throne
That only numbers and great wealth can win?

CREON: Knowest then what must be? Hearken thou shalt
To answering words: and so with knowledge judge.

OEDIPUS: Trickster with words I know thee—yet am I
Not quickly taught, knowing thy deadly hate.

CREON: First hear from me one word that I shall speak.

OEDIPUS: So be thou'lt not assert thou art not base.

CREON: And thou conceive some gain in stubbornness
Unyoked with wisdom, then thou art not wise.

OEDIPUS: And thou conceive escape from punishment,
Doing a kinsman ill, thou art not wise.

CREON: Therein thou speakest true, I grant it thee;
Yet show what wrong from me thou hast endured.

OEDIPUS: Didst thou advise or not that I must send
To fetch forthwith this prophesying priest?

CREON: Aye and now too approve such policy.

OEDIPUS: How long ago was it that Laius hence—

30

CREON: Did what? I follow not thy questioning.

OEDIPUS: Was spirited by fatal violence?

CREON: Long span of years must fill that reckoning.

OEDIPUS: And was this priest a priest in those days too?

CREON: As wise as now and honored equally.

OEDIPUS: Made he then any mention of my name?

CREON: He did not—or at least when I was nigh.

OEDIPUS: And of the murdered king—made ye no search?

CREON: Assuredly we searched but learned no clue.

OEDIPUS: Why then did not this wise man speak these things?

CREON: I know not; knowing not I hold my tongue.

OEDIPUS: This much thou knowest and wouldst be wise to speak.

CREON: What thing? For if I know it, I'll not deny.

OEDIPUS: That had Teiresias not conferred with thee
           He had not named me Laius' murderer.

CREON: If he says so, thou knowest. I too have right
           To question thee as thou hast questioned me.

OEDIPUS: Ask what thou wilt: thou shalt not prove my guilt.

CREON: How then, hast thou my sister for thy wife?

OEDIPUS: That question surely may not be denied.

CREON: And dost thou rule on equal terms with her?

OEDIPUS: All that her heart desires she has from me.

CREON: And am I not a third with equal power?

OEDIPUS: Thou art in truth and so art proven base.

CREON: Nay, if thou usest reason with thyself
Consider first: would any choose to rule
Encompassed round with terror if the same
Authority might rest in perfect peace?
For I at any rate have never sought
To be a king rather than have the right
Of kingly powers—nor any man of sense.
And now from thee with naught to terrify
I have all favor; ruled I here alone
Much must I do perforce against my will.
How then should any crown appear to me
Sweeter than royal privilege secure?
Not yet am I so foolish as to seek
For other goal than honor linked with gain.
Now all men greet me, all men wish me well
And those that would reach thee, bespeak my ear
Since there alone lies prospect of success.
Why then should I abandoning the sure
Advantage that is mine, seek otherwhere?
No mind that harbors wisdom can be false.
And I have neither loved folly myself
Nor could I join another in such act.
Wherefore send now to Pytho for the proof
Of these my words: find out the oracle:
Ask if I told it true. And furthermore
If thou canst prove that with Teiresias
I ever have connived, then not with one
But with a twofold vote, thine own and mine,
Take me and slay me. Only charge me not
In secret with dark counsels. Justice ne'er
Lightly deems bad men good or good men bad.
To cast away a faithful friend I deem
No wiser than to fling aside one's life.
This truth in time thou'lt learn, since time alone

Reveals the just. A single passing day
Amply suffices to disclose the base.

CHORUS: Wise words, my lord, for one that would not slip;
The swift in counsel rarely counsel best.

OEDIPUS: When he who plots in secret moves apace
I too must counsel swiftly. Else my ends,
The while I linger sleeping foolishly,
Are lost forever, his forever gained.

CREON: What wilt thou then? Wouldst drive me from the land?

OEDIPUS: That least of all: my will is death not flight,
Proclaiming to the world base envy's power.

CREON: These are the words of stubborn unbelief.

OEDIPUS: Thou hast not acted to inspire belief.

CREON: Thou seemst not sane.

OEDIPUS: Yet am in my affairs.

CREON: Thou shouldst be so in mine.

OEDIPUS: But thou art base.

CREON: What if thou knowest naught?

OEDIPUS: Yet must I rule.

CREON: Not if thy rule be wrong.

OEDIPUS: O city mine!

CREON: Not thine alone—for Thebes is mine as well.

CHORUS: Desist, my lords. Most happily for you
I see Jocasta coming from the house.
Her help should end this present quarreling.

(*Enter Jocasta.*)

JOCASTA:	What foolish strife of words, all ill-advised,
	Is this ye raise? Are ye not then ashamed,
	Your country perishing, to air abroad
	Your private wrongs? Nay, rather come within
	Nor magnify your petty difference.
CREON:	Nay sister, for thy husband Oedipus
	Makes twofold threat against me—either death
	By violence or exile from this land.
OEDIPUS:	'Tis so for, woman, with base treachery
	I caught him plotting ill against my life.
CREON:	Never may joy be mine but death accursed
	If I am guilty of thy lightest charge.
JOCASTA:	Now by the gods believe him, Oedipus,
	For his oath's sake that he has sworn and for
	My sake as well and these that stand by thee.
CHORUS:	Yield thee, my King, hearken I pray.
OEDIPUS:	What is thy will?
CHORUS:	Grant him belief, wise hitherto, pledging his oath.
OEDIPUS:	Knowest thou what thou wilt?
CHORUS:	Aye.
OEDIPUS:	Then declare it me.
CHORUS:	Never should friend by friend, sworn under oath,
	Lightly be thrust aside.
OEDIPUS:	Know then assuredly asking of me this boon
	Exile for me or death
	Follows thy prayer.
CHORUS:	Nay by the god of light
	By Helios' self, first of the gods above,

May I in misery
Friendless of god and man
Wretchedly die,
If in my inmost breast lurks such desire.
Yearns now my sorrowing heart
Torn by my country's plight
Mocked by thy strife.

OEDIPUS: Let him then go, even though it mean my death
Or if dishonored into banishment
I must depart. Thy words, not his, prevail.
For him where'er he be my hate pursues.

CREON: Grudging is thy surrender, arrogant
Thy wrath. Natures like thine by Fate's decree
Are ever to themselves hardest to bear.

OEDIPUS: Wilt thou not leave me and begone?

CREON: I go.
Thou canst not comprehend—these know me just.

(*Exit Creon.*)

CHORUS: Why, O my Queen, why dost delay?
Lead him within.

JOCASTA: First I must know what hath entailed strife such as this.

CHORUS: Groundless suspicion here: rankling injustice there.

JOCASTA: Nurtured by both?

CHORUS: Aye.

JOCASTA: And the cause?

CHORUS: More than enough to me
Seems now the harm that's done, while yet my country
bleeds.

OEDIPUS: Seest thou then thy zeal
Whither it leads?

CHORUS: Not only once, my King—
I say again, fool should I be and worse
Witless and reft of sense
Should I be false to thee
Thou that didst come
Bringing new life to me, saving the state
Tossed on a raging sea
Aye and again to be
Savior and guide.

JOCASTA: Tell me, my lord, I charge thee by the gods,
Whence came to thee this wrath unquenchable?

OEDIPUS: Thee will I tell—I love thee more than these—
'Twas Creon and his plots against my life.

JOCASTA: Speak plainly if indeed thou hast plain cause.

OEDIPUS: He plainly names me Laius' murderer.

JOCASTA: Speaking his own words or some other man's?

OEDIPUS: Making a bastard priest spokesman for him
To keep unsoiled his own lips, craftily.

JOCASTA: Then think no more of it—hearken to me
And know that never yet hath mortal man
Shared in prophetic art. I'll show to thee
Sure proof of these my words. There came of old
A prophecy to Laius, I say not
From Phoebus' self but from his ministers,
How death should come to him by his son's hand
That should be born to Laius and to me.
Yet—so the rumor hath it—Laius died
Murdered by robbers—strangers—where forsooth
The triple crossroads meet. That child of ours

Not three days old, its ankles bound with thongs,
By others' hands, Laius had left exposed
Far on the trackless hillside. So, I ween,
Apollo did not make of that poor child
His father's murderer nor did fulfill
The fears of Laius that his fate should come
At his child's hand. So did the words of priests
Foretell. Give them no heed. For what god needs
He can himself most easily disclose.

OEDIPUS: What restless thoughts of terror, O my wife
Hast thou engendered in my troubled mind?

JOCASTA: What hath disturbed thee that thou speakest so?

OEDIPUS: Methought I heard thee say that Laius' death
O'ertook him where the triple crossroads meet.

JOCASTA: So ran the story and hath never ceased.

OEDIPUS: Where is the spot that saw the murder done?

JOCASTA: Phocis the land is called—a branching road
Leads there from Delphi and from Daulia.

OEDIPUS: How long the time from that event till now?

JOCASTA: 'Twas just before thy coming that the word
Was brought to us—ere thou wast King of Thebes.

OEDIPUS: O Zeus, what is thy will to do with me?

JOCASTA: Why, Oedipus, should this so trouble thee?

OEDIPUS: Ask me not yet—but tell me this instead.
Laius, what was his form, what years were his?

JOCASTA: His stature tall, silver just streaked his hair,
And in appearance not unlike to thee.

OEDIPUS: Woe, woe, is me: it seems that I have hurled,

37

Unwitting, dreadful curses on myself.

JOCASTA: How sayest; my lord, I tremble at thy word.

OEDIPUS: I fear in truth Teiresias still hath sight.
But thou mayst show. Tell me this one thing more.

JOCASTA: I tremble, yet I'll answer and thou wilt.

OEDIPUS: Did Laius go alone, or like a king,
Surrounded by his spearmen royally?

JOCASTA: Five men in all, a herald one, the King
Rode in his chariot, the rest afoot.

OEDIPUS: Alas, 'tis all too clear. Who was the man
That here returning made report to thee?

JOCASTA: A servant that escaped, alone of all.

OEDIPUS: And now perchance is in the palace here?

JOCASTA: Not so, for when he came to Thebes and found
Thee on the throne, with Laius dead, he pled,
Seizing my hand, to be dispatched far hence
Into the fields, the pastures of our flocks,
That so he might not see the city more.
And I consented. Faithful service given
Deserved such favor, aye and greater too.

OEDIPUS: Might someone bring him here without delay?

JOCASTA: 'Tis possible. Why dost thou wish it so?

OEDIPUS: I fear that I have spoken overmuch.
And for this reason I would see the man.

JOCASTA: The man shall come anon, yet O my lord,
I too deserve to know what troubles thee.

OEDIPUS: Nor shalt thou be denied when such dread fear
Possesses me. For whither should I turn

If not to thee, fast in misfortune's clutch?
My father was King Polybus, the lord
Of Corinth, and my mother Merope.
Dorian she. And I was held the first
Of all the citizens, till there befell
A chance surprising yet not meriting
My great concern thereat. A banqueter
Befuddled with much wine, hurled in my face
The taunt that I was not my father's son.
Much angered, for that day I held my peace
Though hardly: on the next I questioned straight
My parents both who flamed with instant wrath
At him who spake the insult. From their scorn
I took some comfort, but anon the taunt
Rankled unceasing, while the rumor spread.
Wherefore without their knowledge I betook
Myself to Pytho. Whence, touching the quest
That brought me thither, Phoebus caring naught
Sent me away unanswered, yet himself
Vouchsafing other knowledge, bade me know
Dread horror past believing: 'twas my fate
By wedlock with my mother to beget
Offspring abhorrent in the eyes of all
Mankind and be besides the murderer
Of mine own father. When I heard these words
Guided by heaven's stars I fled apace
Corinth and all her land that so I might
Escape fulfilment of the oracle.
Making my way I came unto the spot
Where thou dost say this King of thine was slain.
The truth I'll tell thee, for thou art my wife:
Nearing this triple crossways as I went,
A herald met me and a traveler
Drawn in a carriage, as thou saidst, by colts.

Straightway the herald and the old man too
Were both for pushing me aside. I struck
In righteous anger at the charioteer
Who jostled me; the old man when he saw,
Watching the moment when I passed him close,
Reached from the car and with his two-pronged goad
Smote me upon the head. Unequally
He paid that debt, for with quick reckoning
Struck by the staff in this my hand, he plunged
Headlong from out the chariot. All the rest
I killed, forthwith. Now if there chanced to be
Twixt Laius and this stranger any bond
Of kinship, who in all this wretched world
More wretched than myself? What man more cursed:
Whom not a soul may welcome in the home,
Stranger nor friend, nor speak a word to me
But all must thrust me out. No other man
Invoked this curse but I myself decreed
Such things against myself. The dead man's couch
I have polluted with the self-same hands
That slew him. Am I cursed in very truth?
Am I not all unholy? I must flee
And fleeing may not look upon my own
Nor tread the pathways of my fatherland,
Fearing that Fate foretold, that I should wed
My mother and become the murderer
Of Polybus my father who begat
And reared me. Surely one may well believe
'Tis from some cruel god that on my head
Such fate hath fallen. Never, O gods above
August and holy, never may I see
That day. Rather from sight of all mankind
May I be hidden far, nor e'er behold
The stain of such a doom clinging to me.

CHORUS: Dreadful to me, my lord, these things, yet till
Thou hearest from that witness, nurse thy hope.

OEDIPUS: So much of hope is all that's left me now:
To await the herdsman and to hear his tale.

JOCASTA: And when he comes, what wouldst thou hear from him?

OEDIPUS: I'll tell thee: if his story still remain
Consistent with thine own, then I am cleared.

JOCASTA: What word of mine hath so impressed thee then?

OEDIPUS: By thine account he said in telling thee
Robbers killed Laius. If he still persist
Nor change the number, then I killed him not.
For one and many tally not; but if
He now maintain 'twas but a single man
Surely the deed can only be mine own.

JOCASTA: Nay but he told it so, be well assured,
Nor can deny it now, the city heard,
Not I alone. And if he now deny
Or change his story, he can never prove
That Laius' murder came as prophesied.
Since Loxias said that by his own son's hand
Laius must die. And surely 'twas not he,
That wretched child, that slew him. Nay, himself
Did perish long before. Wherefore henceforth
I'll look not here nor there for oracles.

OEDIPUS: Just is thy reasoning. Yet do not fail
To give thine orders that the peasant come.

JOCASTA: I'll send in haste, but let us go within—
Naught would I do that fits not with thy will.

(Exeunt Oedipus and Jocasta.)

41

Strophe 1

CHORUS: Come whensoe'er it will may Fate o'ertake me still
Guarding each word and act with reverent awe
For swift are the laws of Fate
That have fared from heaven's gate
And god on Olympus' height hath made each law.
No mortal brought them forth, no lethal breath
Awaits them: hall-marked with divinity they know not
  death.

Antistrophe 1

But arrogance breeds force, swift on its course
When glutted full, proud arrogance climbs high,
Snatches the cornice—then, clutching foothold in vain
Plunges, far down on heartless crags to lie.
But the strife that leads to good I shall ever ask,
And to god who rules on high perform my task.

Strophe 2

Whosoe'er in word or deed
Acts with arrogance
Whoso will not justice heed,
Godward looks askance,
Him may justice overtake
Him may Fate unhappy shake
If he get not gain with praise
If he keep not all his ways
Pure from stain of guilt.
Else why this offering here of love,
This worship of dance to the gods above?

Antistrophe 2

Never again to Delphi's shrine
Shall I go with heart's desire,
Never again to Abbae's pine
Nor Olympus' altar fire,
If there be not here
Such music clear
As proveth divinity.
But O thou god if thou hearest aught,
Thou Zeus that rulest on high,
May our impious acts with evil wrought
Scape not thy watchful eye.
For the prophet's word
By our dead King heard,
With holy horror fraught,
Has vanished like air
And Apollo's care,
Is held as naught.

(Enter Jocasta, bearing garlands.)

JOCASTA: Lords of this land, my purpose is resolved
To visit now the temples of the gods
Bearing this wreath and gifts for sacrifice.
For Oedipus' emotions run too high
Beneath his sufferings. Not like a man
Of wisdom doth he judge these new events
By what is old, yielding to each new voice
So be it speak of terrors. Therefore, since
My counseling is vain, to thee I come,
Lycian lord Apollo, suppliant,
(For thou art nearest) to petition thee:
Grant us release without defilement: now

Terror possesses us as who behold
Smitten with fear the captain of their ship.

(*Enter a Messenger.*)

MESSENGER: Strangers I fain would learn from you where dwells
King Oedipus—or better, where is he?

CHORUS: Here stands his palace and himself within.
This is his wife, the mother of his brood.

MESSENGER: Happy be she forever, may she dwell
Always in happiness, being his Queen.

JOCASTA: Blessed be thy lot to whoe'er thou art
For so thy words deserve. But speak: wherefore
Dost thou now come: what news wouldst thou impart?

MESSENGER: Good news unto this house and to the King.

JOCASTA: What is it and from whom thine embassy?

MESSENGER: From Corinth, and the word that I shall speak
Shall bring thee happiness, and grief as well.

JOCASTA: What word is that that hath such twofold power?

MESSENGER: The dwellers of the Isthmian land will make
Him King of Corinth, so the rumor ran.

JOCASTA: How so? Is not old Polybus their king?

MESSENGER: Nay, for Death holds him fast within the tomb.

JOCASTA: How sayest thou? Is Polybus then dead?

MESSENGER: If I speak not the truth then let me die.

JOCASTA: Maiden, run swift and tell thy master this.
Where are ye then, ye oracles of god?
This was the man that, long since, Oedipus

Feared and avoided lest he be constrained
To murder him, and now the self-same King
Lies dead, outdone by Fate and not by him.

(Enter Oedipus.)

OEDIPUS: O dearest wife, Jocasta, why, I pray
Hast thou now summoned me from out the house?

JOCASTA: Hearken to this man's word, then judge thyself
The outcome of the dreaded oracles.

OEDIPUS: Who is the man? What would he say to me?

JOCASTA: Coming from Corinth he brings messages
Of Polybus thy father, and his death.

OEDIPUS: How sayest thou stranger, speak now for thyself.

MESSENGER: If this must be my first report then know
That he has gone indeed the way of Death.

OEDIPUS: By violence, or died he by disease?

MESSENGER: Slight matters turn the scale when one is old.

OEDIPUS: Illness it was then that brought him low.

MESSENGER: Aye, and the long long tale of passing years.

OEDIPUS: Alas, alas, why therefore O my wife
Should one look ever to the Pythian shrine
Or hearken to the cry of birds? 'Twas they
That would have made me murderer of him
My father, yet it seems he now is dead
While here I stand unarmed and innocent—
Unless he died of longing for his son:
So only could one blame me. And in truth
Polybus lies in Hades and hath swept
With him the oracles and proved them naught.

JOCASTA: And said I not long since it would be so?

OEDIPUS: Thou didst, and yet by fear I was misled.

JOCASTA: Now therefore give them not a single thought.

OEDIPUS: Surely I still must fear my mother's couch.

JOCASTA: What fear should be for mortal man whose life
Fate rules supreme, nor can he aught foresee?
Better to live by chance as best ye may.
Nor shouldst thou fear this wedlock horrible
With thine own mother: many men there be
That in their dreams have done this act. He best
Supports his life who counts these things as naught.

OEDIPUS: Well spoken were thy words save that she lives
Who bore me: since she lives she still compels
Terror in me, fair though thy counselings.

JOCASTA: And yet thy father's death should give thee pause.

OEDIPUS: 'Tis true I grant thee, but my mother lives.

MESSENGER: What woman is it whom thou fearest so?

OEDIPUS: Merope, who was wife to Polybus.

MESSENGER: And what the fear that she inspires in thee?

OEDIPUS: An oracle that came, stranger, from god.

MESSENGER: Mayst tell it, or must others know it not?

OEDIPUS: Truly I may. Loxias spoke of old
How I must marry with my mother, then
Shed with these hands of mine, my father's blood.
Corinth and I have therefore been long since
Strangers and happily too save that it's sweet
To look on those who brought us to the light.

MESSENGER: Such was the fear that wrought thy banishment?

OEDIPUS: Aye, that I might not work my father's death.

MESSENGER: How then have I not freed thee from thy fear
Coming, my lord, with welcome messages?

OEDIPUS: And truly thou shalt have thy just reward.

MESSENGER: I will confess that was my secret hope
That I might profit by thy coming home.

OEDIPUS: Home will I never come while she yet lives.

MESSENGER: My son, 'tis clear thou knowest not what thou dost.

OEDIPUS: How so, old man? Tell me now by the gods.

MESSENGER: If for this cause thou wilt not now return.

OEDIPUS: 'Tis cause enough, lest Phoebus prove his word.

MESSENGER: And from thy parents thou incur some guilt?

OEDIPUS: Just so, for that shall always be my fear.

MESSENGER: Dost know, then, that thy fears are all for naught?

OEDIPUS: How can that be and I a child of theirs?

MESSENGER: For Polybus was never kin of thine.

OEDIPUS: What sayest thou? Polybus not my sire?

MESSENGER: No more than I myself, as much, no more.

OEDIPUS: Why match thyself with him who caused my birth?

MESSENGER: Nay, he begat thee not, nor he nor I.

OEDIPUS: Wherefore if this be so, called he me son?

MESSENGER: Delivered by these hands, a gift thou wert.

OEDIPUS: And could he love me so when gotten thus?

MESSENGER: He could by virtue of long childlessness.

OEDIPUS: Thou, hadst thou bought me or didst find this gift?

MESSENGER: I found thee in Cithaeron's wooded glades.

OEDIPUS: Purposing what didst wander to this land?

MESSENGER: In charge of flocks that ranged these mountainsides.

OEDIPUS: Thou wert a shepherd and a hireling then?

MESSENGER: My son, I was thy savior in those days.

OEDIPUS: How so, what suffering didst thou save me from?

MESSENGER: Whereof thine ankles give thee evidence.

OEDIPUS: Alas, why call to mind that ancient woe?

MESSENGER: I loosed thine ankles fastened with a thong.

OEDIPUS: An outrage from my days in swaddling clothes.

MESSENGER: And from that outrage thou hast still thy name.

OEDIPUS: Speak, by the gods; was that a parent's deed?

MESSENGER: I know not, he knows best that gave thee me.

OEDIPUS: Thou didst not find me? I was given thee?

MESSENGER: Another shepherd placed thee in my hands.

OEDIPUS: What man is that? Dost know? Canst point him out?

MESSENGER: 'Twas one of Laius' shepherds, so 'twas said.

OEDIPUS: His who was King in Thebes in days gone by?

MESSENGER: Aye his indeed, a herdsman of that King.

OEDIPUS: Lives the man still that I might look on him?

MESSENGER: Ye men of Thebes should know that best of all.

OEDIPUS: Knows any man of you of whom he speaks
Or have ye seen this shepherd in the town

Or on the upland pastures? Let such speak.
The time is come that these things be revealed.

CHORUS: Methinks it is no other than the man
Thou has desired to see. Jocasta now
Surely might best reveal to thee the truth.

OEDIPUS: O wife and Queen, knowest thou whom but now
We summoned hither? Speaks he of the same?

JOCASTA: What matters whom he mentioned? Give no thought
To what he said, for all such thoughts are vain.

OEDIPUS: It may not be. With such proofs in my grasp
I must discover now my lineage.

JOCASTA: No by the gods, if thou hast any care
For thine own life, ask not. My woe's enough.

OEDIPUS: Fear not, for though from triple servitude
I find my line thou shalt not so be base.

JOCASTA: Believe me none the less: touch not this thing.

OEDIPUS: I may not so believe thee, I must learn.

JOCASTA: For thine own sake I speak and counsel well.

OEDIPUS: These counselings have long since vexed my soul.

JOCASTA: O hapless man, god grant thee ignorance.

OEDIPUS: Let someone bring this shepherd to me straight:
This woman, let her boast her royal line.

JOCASTA: Alas, most wretched man; for this one word
I speak thee now, none else forevermore.

(*Exit Jocasta.*)

CHORUS: Why has she gone, thy Queen, O Oedipus,

In frenzied grief? I fear that from this deep
Silence of hers misfortune shall break forth.

OEDIPUS: Let come what will. Low though my lineage
Be proven, yet I'll know it. She perchance
Womanlike in her pride may fear in shame
To face mine origin. I hold myself
Own child of Fortune; she beneficent
Shall never cause me shame. Her child am I
Brother of all the months whose passing course
Made me now small now great and being such
In parentage pray god I never prove
False to that mother Fortune nor desert
The search that shall yet prove my lineage.

Strophe

CHORUS: Now by Olympus high
If aught of prophecy
          Or wisdom lie
          Within this breast
Tomorrow's moon shall see
          Our Oedipus stand confessed
Thy countryman, Cithaeron, and thy son,
          This dance a duty done
                    In loyalty.
Lord god, Apollo, let these our deeds be blessed.

Antistrophe 2

Whose was the goddess' womb
That unto Pan bore thee
          Through wooded coomb
          And grass-grown, run
Pursued relentlessly?

50

Or art thou Apollo's son?
For dear to him is every upland way.
Or Hermes'—who shall say?
Or was it he
Great Bacchus loved of the nymphs on Helicon?

(Enter a Herdsman.)

OEDIPUS: Sir, if I too who never met the man,
May yet venture a guess, yonder, methinks
I see the herdsman whom we seek. In years
He matches well this stranger and besides
Servants they are of mine conducting him.
Yet better is thy knowledge than mine own
Since thou hast seen the fellow ere today.

CHORUS: I know him, have no doubt, of Laius' men
Shepherd of all most faithful to the King.

OEDIPUS: Thee first I question; didst thou mean this man,
Stranger from Corinth?

MESSENGER: Aye, the man thou seest.

OEDIPUS: Thou too old man, look hither, answer me
My question: wast thou ever Laius' man?

HERDSMAN: I was, a house-born slave, no market prize.

OEDIPUS: What task was thine? How didst thou spend thy life?

HERDSMAN: The larger part in following the herds.

OEDIPUS: What were the regions thou didst most frequent?

HERDSMAN: Cithaeron mostly and its neighborhood.

OEDIPUS: This fellow here, hast ever seen him there?

HERDSMAN: What doing, sir, and what man dost thou mean?

OEDIPUS: Who stands before thee: hast met him before?

HERDSMAN: Not so that I might say at once from memory.

MESSENGER: Nor any wonder. Yet, my lord, I can
Clearly recall what now he has forgot.
I doubt not he remembers well the time
When for three summers clear from spring until
Arcturus' rising we together roamed
These stretches of Cithaeron, he with two
Herds while I tended one. When winter came
I drove my flocks to Corinth home, he his
To Laius' folds. Is this the truth I speak
Or do I tell of things that never were?

HERDSMAN: The truth indeed, and yet 'twas long ago.

MESSENGER: Come tell me then, canst thou recall how once
Thou gavest me a child to rear as mine?

HERDSMAN: How now? Why dost thou question me of that?

MESSENGER: For this is he who was a baby then.

HERDSMAN: Destruction take thee, wilt thou hold thy tongue?

OEDIPUS: Old man, revile him not, thy words not his
Seem most to need amendment, chide him not.

HERDSMAN: And what, good master, have I done amiss?

OEDIPUS: Refusing thus to answer what he asks.

HERDSMAN: He asks in ignorance, and all in vain.

OEDIPUS: Thou speak not freely, thou shalt speak in pain.

HERDSMAN: By all the gods, force not an aged man.

OEDIPUS: Will someone quickly bind the fellow's hands?

HERDSMAN: Ah wretched me, for what, what wouldst thou know?

OEDIPUS: The child, didst give it to him as he says?

HERDSMAN: I did, and would to god I had died then.

OEDIPUS: Thou shalt die now and thou speak not the truth.

HERDSMAN: And if I do, more surely shall I die.

OEDIPUS: The fellow seems determined to delay.

HERDSMAN: Not I, I told you that I gave the child.

OEDIPUS: Whence had thou it, was't thine or someone's else?

HERDSMAN: 'Twas not mine own, I had it from a man.

OEDIPUS: A Theban? One of these? And from what home?

HERDSMAN: No, by the gods, my lord, ask me no more.

OEDIPUS: Thou art a dead man if I ask again.

HERDSMAN: Well then it was a child of Laius' house.

OEDIPUS: A slave, or one free born of his own race?

HERDSMAN: Alas I tremble on the brink of speech.

OEDIPUS: And I of hearing, yet perforce, I must.

HERDSMAN: His own the child was called. The Queen within
Thy wife may best confirm to thee the fact.

OEDIPUS: Was it she gave the child?

HERDSMAN: 'Twas she, my lord.

OEDIPUS: What was her purpose?

HERDSMAN: I should kill the child.

OEDIPUS: Unnatural mother.

HERDSMAN: Oracles she feared.

OEDIPUS: What?

HERDSMAN: He should kill his parent, so 'twas said.

OEDIPUS: How then didst thou bestow him on this man?

HERDSMAN: In pity, sire, thinking that he would take
The child to his own country, yet it seems
He saved him to misfortune. If thou art
The man he says, then dreadful is thy doom.

OEDIPUS: Alas, alas. It must then all be true.
O light of day, may I ne'er look on thee
Again, who now am found cursed at my birth,
Wedded in incest, steeped in mine own blood.

(*Exeunt.*)

Strophe 1

CHORUS: Alas, alas for the years of mortality:
I count ye as naught.
Who is he that hath ever found
More than a vision of empty sound
By fancy wrought?
And ever the vision ends in calamity.
For now, my King, soul wracked and sore distressed,
Thy fate do I behold
Woes manifold
And I count no mortal blessed.

Antistrophe 1

Beyond man's skill did he speed his unerring shaft
And won to his goal
Fortune's prize of prosperity
Slaying the Sphinx with her mystery
And stopped the toll

54

Of that death she levied: foully she wrought and laughed
    Till thou didst come, champion and tower of might.
        Henceforth all conquering
          Art hailed as king
      In this land of god's delight.

Strophe 2

And now on the lips of all
    Whose fate so black?
While the Furies of madness in hungry pack
    Cry for thy fall.
For into a harbor strange thou hast sailed
Where the deathless laws of the gods have failed,
Where the same unhallowed love prevailed
On sire and son in the self-same hall.
    What god bestowed
This poisonous boon, this fatal goad
    To sow where his father sowed?

Antistrophe 2

But time that is never blind
    Hath now disclosed
What the dwellers of earth, to the light exposed,
    Shudder to find.
Seed of begetter and him begot
In the self-same furrow that sensed them not
And I would to god thy thrice-cursed lot
Were hidden darkly from all mankind.
    I mourn thy plight
That unto me brought sudden light
    To end in eternal night.

(*Enter a Second Messenger.*)

SECOND MESSENGER:	Ye ever-honored most in Thebes what deeds Shall smite your ears, what sights shall ye behold What grief is yours if to tradition true Ye still revere the house of Labdacus. Waters of Ister, streams of Phasis ne'er Can cleanse this dwelling, such the dreadful deed, It hides but shall disclose, no deed of chance But wittingly contrived. Always those griefs Hurt most whose choice the world shall mark our own.
CHORUS:	Already we have witnessed here such deeds As might call forth such cry; what hast thou more?
SECOND MESSENGER:	To take the shortest course for him who speaks And him who hears: the Queen Jocasta is dead.
CHORUS:	O lady of ill fortune, by what means?
SECOND MESSENGER:	By her own hand. The part most horrible, The sight of it, is spared thee. What remains Of all her woe within my memory Straight shalt thou hear. Frantic with mad despair She came within the antechamber. Then Rushed to the wedding couch, with both her hands Tearing her hair, dashed shut the doors behind Invoking Laius, dead these many years, And called to mind that son that he begot So long ago by whom he died and left Her that had borne him wretched to produce Offspring to share with his. She cried against That marriage which to her misfortune raised A double brood, husband by husband got And children by her child. How after that She perished I know not, for Oedipus Burst in with shouting who allowed us not

Further to look upon her misery
Since on his frenzy rested all our eyes.
Madly he raged, asking of us a sword
And calling for the wife that was no wife
The mother's womb that bore alike himself
And his own children. In his madness some
Divinity did guide him for 'twas none
Of us poor mortals who were standing by.
Then with a dreadful shout, as beckoned on
He hurled himself upon the double doors—
Back from their sockets bent the yielding bolts—
And rushed within. There we beheld his wife
Hanged by a twisted cord still swaying there.
And when he saw her, with a mighty cry
He loosed the rope that held her. As she lay
Stretched on the ground, followed a gruesome sight.
For from her dress he tore the golden brooch
That held it. Raising it aloft he smote
Full on his eyeballs shouting as he struck
That they should nevermore behold what he
Had suffered nor the evil he had wrought.
Darkened forever they might never look
Again on what they had no right to see,
Failing to recognize what most they ought.
And with such imprecations 'twas not once
But many times he beat upon his eyes.
The bloody eyeballs burst upon his beard
Not in slow drops of blood but in one black
Down-rushing stream of blood, like shower of hail.
Such are the woes that issue from these twain,
Husband and wife commingled. What was once
Their happy lot, and happiness in truth,
This day is turned to wailing, madness, death
And all the woes that are, are theirs today.

CHORUS: Hath now the wretched man some rest from **pain?**

SECOND
MESSENGER: He shouts aloud that someone draw the bolts
            And show to all in Thebes the murderer
            Of his own father and his mother too.
            With blasphemies that I may not repeat
            He swears to hurl himself forth from this land
            Nor still remain a curse unto the house,
            Under the curse he spoke. Yet someone's strength
            And guidance too he needs, his agony
            Is more than human strength can bear. Thou too
            Shalt see, for now the unbolted palace gates
            Open to show a sight that can but win
            Thy fierce abhorrence but thy pity too.

            (Enter the blinded Oedipus.)

CHORUS: O agony too sore for sight
            Beyond the utmost range
            Of human agony.
            What madness, hapless man, assailed thy soul?
            What angered god
            O'erleaping space
            Struck down thine ill-starred Fortune?
            Woe is me,
            Much as I fain would learn,
            Frozen with horror, impotent,
            I dare not ask nor look but overwhelmed
            Shudder and hold my peace.

OEDIPUS: Woe, woe is mine.
            Where in mine agony
            Shall I be borne?
            Fluttering words are naught.
            Where, god, the end?

CHORUS: Where there is no relief for ear or eye.

OEDIPUS: O cloud of the nether night,
Abhorrent, unspeakable,
Wafted on following breezes fraught with death
Alas the goad of memory strikes
Piercing my heart
Cruelly joined in one with the stabs
Of the golden brooch.

CHORUS: No wonder in thy plight there comes to thee
A double grief, a twofold pain to bear.

OEDIPUS: O friend that art steadfast still
Thou only art left to me.
Pity for suffering blindness makes thee kind.
Alas thy presence speaks to me
Blind though I am.
Darkness like death is mine, yet I know
Thou hast left me not.

CHORUS: O doer of dread deeds, how couldst thou dare
Destroy thine eyes? What god compelled that act?

OEDIPUS: Lord of the Delphian shrine,
Apollo, god of the taut strong bow,
Wrought for me woe on woe:
His was the curse
But the hand that struck was mine;
Mine was the blow.
God! Would I see again
Whose opened eyes
Could naught behold that held not memory's curse?

CHORUS: True is that word of thine.

OEDIPUS: What should I see? Shall I ever know
Love or a welcoming word?

Banish me ere ye too
Fall neath the blight that clings
Round me accursed
Hated of god, damned through eternity.

CHORUS: Twofold thy misery: for, being damned,
Thou still canst feel. Would god I knew thee not.

OEDIPUS: Cursed forever be
The hand that loosed from my feet the thong
Striking the shackles off
Giving me life
When I lay a helpless babe.
Graceless the deed;
Better were death for me
Than live a curse
To mine own self and all that touches me.

CHORUS: Better were death indeed.

OEDIPUS: Then had I not with the curse of god
Drenched in my father's blood
Mounted the couch of her,
Mother and Queen to me.
Outlaw from earth
Outlaw from heaven, woe beyond woe is mine.

CHORUS: I cannot say thy counsel was the best
For death would be to thee a very boon.

OEDIPUS: Instruct me not that all is evilly
Contrived. I cannot bear more counseling
For had I now my sight could I endure
To face my father in the halls of hell,
To look upon my mother? I have wrought
Such wrongs against those two as would make death
By hanging seem as nothing. Can ye think
Beside that sight of mine own progeny

Begotten as they were could give me joy?
Not in mine eyes at least. Not Thebes herself,
Not all her parapets, her sculptured gods
Seeing that I of all her citizens
Fairest of promise, now accursed, have won
The doom of seeing these no more, myself
The spokesman of the curse bidding men thrust
Forth from the city the unholy one,
Disclosed by god of Laius' royal line.
Could I with such a brand upon me look
Upon my fellow citizens? Not I,
And were there means to dam the fountain head
Of hearing, I had not withheld to close
This wretched body fast that neither sight
Nor sound should penetrate. Our thoughts should dwell
Beyond the reach of evil, O Cithaeron, why
Didst thou accept my life? Why didst thou not
Slay me at once? So had I never shown
Myself unto the world and whence I sprang.
O Polybus and Corinth and that home
Once called mine own, how fair the object seemed
Of thy kind nurture, and how foul beneath
Proven at last both base and basely born.
O triple crossroads and that hidden glade
Narrowing through the oak trees where those three
Roads met that drank mine own blood by my hand
Drawn from my father's veins, do ye then still
Remember me, the deed I showed you there
And coming hither wrought again? O rites
Of wedlock, ye that brought me forth and gave
Harvest to me sown in the self-same field
Confounding name of father, brother, son,
Of mother, bride, and wife to consummate
All that is held most shameful of mankind.

61

Yet what is foul to do is foul to speak.
Wherefore by all the gods with utmost speed
Hide me in some far hiding place or slay
Outright or cast me in the sea where none
May e'er behold me more. Come, scruple not
To touch this wretched man. Ye need not fear.
No mortal but myself may bear this guilt.

(*Enter Creon.*)

CHORUS: Lo at thy words comes Creon who may best
Grant thy request or counsel thee for he
Alone is left our guardian in thy place.

OEDIPUS: Alas what word is left for me to speak
To him? What truth shall he behold in me
Who proved myself to him in all things false?

CREON: I am not come to mock thee, Oedipus,
Nor speak reproaches for thy evil past.
But if ye here respect no more the race
Of man at least show reverence to the flame
All nourishing of Helios nor expose
Pollution such as this which neither light
Of day, nor earth, nor rains of heaven may bear.
With all your speed lead him within. The woes
Of kindred they alone should see and hear
To whom the bonds of kinship give the right.

OEDIPUS: Nay, by the gods, since thou hast quelled my fear
Coming thus nobly to a man so base
Grant me one boon. For thine own sake I'll speak.

CREON: What favor dost thou ask so eagerly?

OEDIPUS: Cast me forth swiftly from this land, where I
May share no more in human intercourse.

CREON: That had I done, be well assured, save that
           I would be taught of god what's best to do.

OEDIPUS: God hath already spoken bidding us
           Destroy the unholy man that slew his sire.

CREON: Such was his word yet seeing where we stand
           'Tis best to learn anew our proper course.

OEDIPUS: Wilt ask advice about one so accursed?

CREON: Aye for thyself wilt now believe god's word.

OEDIPUS: One charge I lay on thee, one last request.
           To her that lies within give burial
           As seemeth best to thee. So shalt thou give
           Last rites unto thine own. But never doom
           This city of my fathers to receive
           Me as a citizen to dwell therein.
           Nay send me forth to live where rises steep
           Cithaeron, called mine own, the living tomb
           My father and my mother gave to me:
           Thus at their hands who willed it I may die.
           Yet this I know. Never shall dread disease
           Nor human ill destroy me. I was snatched
           From death, to serve some stranger will of god.
           For me let Fate lead where it will. And more
           I ask no favor, Creon, for my sons.
           They are now men and wheresoe'er they are
           Shall win their livelihood. I crave thy care
           For my two daughters. Piteous is their lot
           Who know no table but mine own, have shared
           All things with me. Grant too, most noble lord,
           That I may touch them once again and mourn
           With them this evil plight. Could I but place
           My hands on them methinks I could believe
           That they were mine as when I saw them here.

(*Enter Antigone and Ismene, Oedipus' daughters.*)

O god what shall I say? Do I not hear
Their weeping voices? Hast thou pitied me
And brought my daughters, Creon? Is it so?

CREON: 'Tis so. 'Twas I that brought them, knowing well
From thy past joy what comfort they might give.

OEDIPUS: God give thee blessing and a happier fate
Than mine for this good act. Where are ye there,
My children? Hither, hither come and take
These hands that are in truth a brother's hands.
Hands which wrought havoc with your father's eyes
That saw so clearly once. Yet seeing naught
Nor gaining wisdom's light, he gave you life
By his own mother. 'Tis for you I weep
Whom now I may not see. But I perceive
What bitterness of life amongst mankind
Henceforth is yours. What friendly gatherings
Will you attend, what feasts whose end for you
Shall not be weeping in the place of joy?
And when you reach the years of womanhood
With thoughts of marriage, who will then assume
Reproaches that must ever fall alike
On my descendants and on yours? What woe
Exists that is not ours? Your father slew
His sire, quickened the womb that gave him life
To bring you forth. Such is your heritage.
Who then shall wed you? There is none that lives.
Unwedden, barren, 'tis your doom to die.
But O Menoeceus' son, since thou alone
Art left to father these—for she and I
That brought them to the light are lost indeed—
Suffer them not—thy kin—to wander lone

64

Beggared and husbandless nor make them one
With this my misery. Nay pity them
Seeing their youth deprived of everything
Save what may come from thee. Take thou this hand
And grant my wish. To you my children much
I should bequeath of counsel were thy minds
Mature. Now let this be your constant prayer
That wheresoe'er chance place your lot, ye live
With happier fate than was your father's share.

CREON: All sufficient now thy mourning. Thou must go within
    the house.

OEDIPUS: Yield I must, though yield I would not.

CREON: Aye, for all things have their time.

OEDIPUS: Knowest how I might go freely?

CREON: If thou sayest I shall know.

OEDIPUS: If thou wouldst but grant me exile.

CREON: That lies on the knees of god.

OEDIPUS: Yet to god am I most hateful.

CREON: Hence may win thy wish perchance.

OEDIPUS: Thou dost will it?

CREON: Nay, 'tis never mine to speak what I mean not.

OEDIPUS: Send me then within the palace.

CREON: Go, but leave thy children here.

OEDIPUS: Rob me not of them I pray thee.

CREON: Seek not to prevail in all.
    For the power thou once hast wielded has not followed to
    the end.

CHORUS: Ye that dwell in Thebes behold him. Oedipus thy King is this,

He who solved the far-famed riddle, mightiest in all Thebes was he.

On his fortune who that dwelt here gazed not once with envious eye?

Now behold what surge of evil hath encompassed him about.

So the while we wait the outcome of the fateful final day

We may call no mortal happy till his course of life is done

And he reach the goal of darkness, find his heaven free from pain.

SOPHOCLES

❖❖❖❖❖❖❖❖❖

Oedipus at Colonus

Translated by E. H. Plumptre

CHARACTERS IN THE PLAY

OEDIPUS

ANTIGONE $\left.\begin{array}{c}\end{array}\right\}$ *daughters of Oedipus*
ISMENE

THESEUS, *king of Athens*

CREON, *a Theban*

POLYNEICES, *the elder son of Oedipus*

ATHENIAN STRANGER

A MESSENGER

CHORUS *of Elders of Colonus*

ARGUMENT

Oedipus had continued to live at Thebes for many years after the conclusion of the events described in Oedipus the King. *Then Creon banished him, with the consent of Oedipus' sons, Eteocles and Polyneices. Eventually Creon ceased to be king, and the two brothers quarreled over the succession. Polyneices fled to Argos, married the daughter of King Adrastus, and has now levied an army to support his pretensions to the Theban throne. Recently an oracle has proclaimed that if Oedipus dies in Attica, Athens will prosper and Thebes suffer: actually, from the religious point of view, the death of the aged and innocent Oedipus, who pleads the venial nature of an offense committed in ignorance although long since purified by his suffering, represents the highest achievement of paganism. As we listen to the Messenger's description of Oedipus' last moments, our souls are in truth lifted toward grandeur.*

68

At Colonus in Attica, a suburb of Athens. In the background is the sacred grove of the Eumenides, or Gentle Powers, a euphemistic title for the Erinyes or Furies. The blind Oedipus, led by his daughter Antigone, enters.

OEDIPUS: Child of a blind old man, Antigone,
    What country reach we? Whose the city near?
    Who will receive the wanderer, Oedipus,
    And give him, day by day, his scanty needs?
    He asks but little; than that little, less
    Most times receiving, finding that enough:
    For I have learnt contentment; chance and change
    Have taught me this, and the long course of time,
    And the stout heart within me. But, my child,
    If that thou see'st a place where I may sit,
    On common ground, or by the groves of Gods,
    There place me; prop me up, that we may learn
    Where now we are. As strangers we have come,
    To learn from those that dwell as townsmen here,
    And what we hear, in all completeness do.

ANTIGONE: My father, woe-worn Oedipus! afar,
    If I see right, are towers that shield a town:
    This spot is holy, one may clearly tell,
    Full as it is of laurel, olive, vine,
    And many a nightingale within sings sweetly.
    Rest thy limbs here upon this rough-hewn rock;
    Long hast thou travelled, for thine age, to-day.

OEDIPUS: Place me then here, and o'er the blind man watch.

(*She leads him to the seat.*)

ANTIGONE: I do not need to learn that lesson now.

OEDIPUS: And can'st thou tell me where we take our stand?

ANTIGONE: Athens, I know; but not this very spot.

OEDIPUS: That every traveller told us, as we came.

ANTIGONE: But shall I go and ask what place it is?

OEDIPUS: Do so, my child, if men inhabit it.

ANTIGONE: Inhabitants there are; and lo! I think
I need not go. One passes by our way.

OEDIPUS: And is he coming this way, hastening here?

ANTIGONE: He is close by; and what thou deem'st it right
To speak in season, say. The man is here.

(*Enter an Athenian Stranger.*)

OEDIPUS: My friend, from this girl hearing, who for me
And for herself doth see, that thou art come
A well-timed guide, to tell us where we doubt. . . .

STRANGER: Before thou speakest further leave thy seat,
For here thou hold'st a place man may not tread.

OEDIPUS: What is the place? To what God consecrate?

STRANGER: Man comes not here, nor dwells. The Goddesses,
Dread daughters of the Earth and Darkness, claim it.

OEDIPUS: What solemn name should I invoke them with?

STRANGER: Eumenides, the Gentle Ones, all seeing,—
They call them here. It may be, other names
Befit them elsewhere.

OEDIPUS: May they then receive me,
Their suppliant, gently: thus I need not go,
Nor ever quit my station on their ground!

STRANGER: What means this?

OEDIPUS: 'Tis the omen of my fate.

STRANGER: And I, too, dare not move thee from thy seat,
Without the state's command, before I tell
My tale, and learn what it is meet to do.

OEDIPUS: By all the Gods, I charge thee scorn me not,
Poor wanderer though I be! But what I ask
I pray thee tell.

STRANGER: Speak, then, thou shalt not meet,
As far as my will goes, with scorn or shame.

OEDIPUS: And what, then, is this place to which we've come?

STRANGER: All that I know thou too shalt hear and learn:
The ground all round is sacred, and the dread
Poseidon claims it, and the God of fire,
Titan Prometheus; and the place thou tread'st on
Is called the brass-paved threshold of our land,
Bulwark of Athens. And the neighbouring fields
Boast they have yon Colonus on his horse
To be their patron; and they bear his name,
All called alike, in honour of their God.
Such, stranger, are our glories, not in words
Shown chiefly, but much more by full resort.

OEDIPUS: And are there any who inhabit here?

STRANGER: Ay, that there are, this God's great name who bear.

OEDIPUS: Is there a chief, or do the people rule?

STRANGER: Our city's king extends his sway to us.

OEDIPUS: And who is this that rules in word and might?

STRANGER: Theseus his name, the child of Aegeus old.

OEDIPUS: Would one of you go fetch him here to me?

STRANGER: Simply to tell, or show him why to come?

OEDIPUS: That he, a little helping, much may gain.

STRANGER: And what help comes there from a man that's blind?

OEDIPUS: The words we speak will see with open eyes.

STRANGER: Know'st thou, my friend, in what way not to err,—
              Noble, as one may see, but for the fate
              That Heaven has laid on thee? Do thou stay here,
              Here where I saw thee, while I go and tell
              The townsmen on this very spot, not there,
              Up in the city. They shall come and judge
              If thou should'st tarry, or go back again.

              (*Exit Athenian Stranger.*)

OEDIPUS: My child, and is the stranger gone from us?

ANTIGONE: He is gone, O my father. Thou may'st speak
              In quiet all things; I alone am near.

OEDIPUS: O dread and awful Beings, since to halt
              On your ground first I bent my wearied limbs,
              Be ye not harsh to Phoebus, and to me;
              For He, when he proclaimed my many woes,
              Told of this respite, after many years;
              When I should reach the bourn of all my life,
              That I should claim a stranger's place, and sit,
              A suppliant at the shrine of dreaded Gods,
              And then should near the goal of woe-worn life,
              To those who should receive me bringing gain;

To those who sent me—yea, who drove me—evil;
And that sure signs should give me pledge of this,
Earthquake, or thunder, or the flash of Zeus.
And now I know full well it cannot be
But faithful omen, sent to me by you,
To this grove brought me. Else I had not first,
Untasting wine, upon my way met you,
E'en you who loathe the wine-cup, nor had sat
On this rough, hallowed seat. But, O ye Powers,
Grant me, according to Apollo's voice,
An issue and completion of my life;
Unless it chance I seem too low for this,
Of all mankind the most enslaved to ills.
Come, ye sweet daughters of the Darkness old,
Come, O thou city bearing Pallas' name,
O Athens, of all cities most renowned,
Have pity on this wasted, spectral form
That once was Oedipus. No longer now
Is this my carcase what it was of old.

ANTIGONE: Hush! for there come this way some reverend men,
To ask the meaning of thy sitting here.

OEDIPUS: I will be silent, and do thou convey
My feet within the grove, till I shall hear
What words they utter; for in learning this
We gather caution in the things we do.

(*Oedipus retires with Antigone into the grove.*)

(*Enter Chorus of Elders of Colonus.*)

Strophe

CHORUS: Look then! Who was it? Where his hiding place?

Where has he fled and rushed,
Of all men boldest found?
Look, search, seek everywhere.
A stranger—yea, a stranger must he be.
No countryman of ours, that blind old man;
     For never else had he
     Approached the holy grove,
     By foot of man untrod,
Where dwell the Virgin Ones invincible,
     Whose names we fear to speak.
Yea, we pass by, and dare not raise our eyes,
     Voiceless and speechless all,
     Uttering the whispered sound
     Of thought that fears to speak.
     But now the rumour spreads
     Of some one hither come,
     Unmoved by touch of awe,
And yet around the precinct all in vain
I search, and fail to find
Where now his foot abides.

(Oedipus shows himself.)

OEDIPUS: I am the man; for by the voice I see,
            As runs the adage.

CHORUS: Ah me! ah me! most dread to look upon,
            Most dread to hear art thou.

OEDIPUS: Do not, I pray you, deem me a transgressor.

CHORUS: Great Zeus, our shield, who may this old man be?

OEDIPUS: Not one to highest place
                 Of fair good fortune born,
                 Ye rulers of the land.

74

This show I all too plain, or had not crept,
    Trusting to others' eyes,
Nor, mighty once, had come to harbour here
With anchors poor and weak.

Antistrophe

CHORUS:
Ah me! ah me! and wast thou born, alas!
    With those poor, sightless eyes!
    Worn out with many a woe,
    And, as one well may guess,
Worn with age too; but for my part, at least,
Thou shalt not bring fresh curses on thyself;
    Too far thou goest, too far.
    But that thou rush not on
    Through voiceless, grass-grown grove,
Where blends with rivulet of honeyed stream,
    The cup of waters clear,
Of this beware, O man, weighed down with woe.
    Bestir thyself, depart;
    The distance hinders us.
Hear'st thou, O wanderer worn?
If thou my speech wilt heed,
Go forth from ground where man's foot may not go,
To where all walk alike.
Then speak; till then abstain.

OEDIPUS:
(To Antigone.) What turn should counsel take, my child, in this?

ANTIGONE:
O father, we to citizens should give
Their due, and yield and hearken as is meet.

OEDIPUS:
Come, then, and touch me.

ANTIGONE:
                Here then is my hand.

(*She leads him out of the grove.*)

OEDIPUS: So then, my friends, I pray,
Let me not suffer wrong,
Trusting thy plighted word,
And moving from my place.

CHORUS: No one from henceforth, 'gainst thy will, old man,
Shall lead thee from this spot.

(*Pointing to a rock near them.*)

OEDIPUS: Still farther on?

CHORUS: Yet onward take thy course.

OEDIPUS: What! farther still?

CHORUS: (*To Antigone.*) Lead him on, maiden, farther,
For thou discernest clear.

ANTIGONE: Follow then, follow, with thy sightless limbs,
My father, where I lead.

CHORUS: A stranger in a land that is not thine,
Endure, O suffering one,
To loathe whate'er our state doth hateful hold,
To reverence what it loves.

OEDIPUS: Lead me then on, my child,
Where, on due reverence resting,
We may both speak and hear;
Nor let us war with fate.

CHORUS: Stop here; nor farther bend thy foot
Beyond this platform hewn from out the rock.

OEDIPUS: Shall it be thus?

CHORUS: Enough, as now thou hearest.

OEDIPUS: And may I sit?

CHORUS: Just leaning sideways here,
On the rock's edge sit low and bend thy knees.

ANTIGONE: This, father, be my task. With gentle tread,
        Step after step advance;

        (*Oedipus groans.*)

Thy agèd frame to my fond hand confide.

OEDIPUS: Ah me! my weary fate!

CHORUS: O suffering one, since now thou givest way,
        Speak. Who of mortals art thou?
    Who are thou that art led thus miserable?
        Thy country we would learn.

OEDIPUS: I am an exile, friends; but no! not that—

CHORUS: And why, old man, why shrinkest thou from that?

OEDIPUS: No! no! let no one ask me who I am:
    Search not, with over-curious, idle quest.

CHORUS: What means all this?

OEDIPUS: My birth was terrible.

CHORUS: Yet tell it out!

OEDIPUS: (*To Antigone.*) What must I say, my child?

CHORUS: Tell us, O stranger, of what race thou com'st?

OEDIPUS: Woe! woe! What sorrow comes on me, my child!

ANTIGONE: Tell them, for thou art in a sore strait now.

OEDIPUS: Yea, I will speak. No hiding-place is left.

CHORUS: Ye linger long; make haste to tell thy tale.

OEDIPUS: Know ye of Laius' son?

CHORUS: Ah woe! ah woe!

OEDIPUS: The race of the Labdacidae?

CHORUS: O Zeus!

OEDIPUS: The wretched Oedipus?

CHORUS: And art thou he?

OEDIPUS: Yet fear thou nothing, whatsoe'er I say.

CHORUS: Alas! alas!

OEDIPUS: O miserable me!

CHORUS: Woe! woe!

OEDIPUS: My daughter! what befalls us now?

CHORUS: Depart ye from our land!

OEDIPUS: And wilt thou thus thy promise to us keep?

CHORUS: Vengeance comes not from Heaven on any man,
Avenging wrongs that men have done to him;
But fraud on this side meeting fraud on that,
Repays with pain, not kindness. Go, I say,
From this spot too; forth from my land depart,
Lest on my city some fresh ill thou bring.

ANTIGONE: O strangers, kind and pitiful of heart,
　　　　Since ye could not endure
　　To hear my agèd father speak of crimes
　　　　Done most unwillingly;
　　Have pity, I implore you, friends, on me,
　　Who for my lonely father supplicate—
　　Yea, supplicate, with eyes not blind and dark,

Gazing on thine eyes, as a maiden might,
    Who common kindred claimed,
That at your hands this old man, woe-begone,
May find the pity that is born of awe.
On you, as on a god, we rest our fate;
But grant, oh, grant me this unlooked-for boon.
By all that is most dear, I supplicate,
Thy child, thy wife, thy treasure, or thy God;
Search where thou wilt, thou ne'er wilt find a man
With strength to 'scape when God shall lead him on.

CHORUS: Know, child of Oedipus, we pity thee,
And him too, for your sad calamity;
But, fearing God, we may not dare to speak
One word beyond the orders thou hast heard.

OEDIPUS: What profit is there then of noble fame,
Or fair report all idly floating on,
If men can speak of Athens, most devout,
The one deliverer of the stranger-guest,
When wronged or injured, yea, his one support?
What is all this to me, whom ye did raise
From where I stood, and then drive out by force,
Fearing my name alone? It cannot be
Ye fear my presence or my deeds; for they
Were rather suffered by me than performed,
If I must tell thee what befell my parents,
On whose account thou dread'st me. This I know.
And yet how was I base and vile of heart?
For I did but requite the wrongs I suffered,
So that, not even had I done the deed
With open eyes, should I be guilty found.
But, as it was, I, knowing nothing, went
Just where I went, while they who wronged me sought,
Well knowing it, my death. And therefore, friends,

I pray ye, by the Gods, as ye have raised me,
So now deliver, nor, with outward show
Honouring the Gods, then count the Gods as nought;
But think that they behold the godly soul,
Beholding too the godless: never yet
Was refuge found for impious child of man.
And therefore shame not Athens, blest of God,
Lending thy hands to any impious deeds;
But, as thou did'st receive me as a suppliant,
And give me pledge of safety, free me now;
Free me and guard, and look not thou with scorn
On this grey head, so foul to look upon.
For I am come, as sacred, fearing God,
Bringing this people profit. And your lord,
When he shall come, whom ye your ruler call,
Then thou shalt hear and know the whole. Meanwhile,
Be not thou found as base in anything.

CHORUS: I needs must feel some shrinking as I hear,
Old man, thy reasonings, for with no slight words
Have they been uttered. 'Tis enough for me
That they who rule us search the matter out.

OEDIPUS: And where, my friends, is he who rules this land?

CHORUS: He keeps his father's city. But the scout
Who sent me here, is gone to summon him.

OEDIPUS: And think ye he will any pity feel,
Or care for me, the blind one, and will come?

CHORUS: Right sure am I, when once he hears thy name.

OEDIPUS: And who is he that will report it to him?

CHORUS: The way is long; but market news is wont
To wander fast. And when he hears the news,
Be of good cheer, he'll come. For know, old man,

80

Thy name has come to all men, and though slow
His speed at first, yet hearing, he will haste.

OEDIPUS: And may he come with blessing to his country,
And to me also! Who that lives is found
Unfriendly to himself?

ANTIGONE: (*Starting.*) Zeus! What is this?
My father! whither shall I turn my thoughts?

OEDIPUS: What is 't my child, Antigone?

(*Ismene is seen in the distance.*)

ANTIGONE: I see
Advancing near us, mounted on a colt
Of Aetna's breed, a woman's form. Her head
Is shaded by a broad Thessalian hat.
What shall I say? . . And can it be? . . 'Tis not.—
Does my mind cheat me? Now 'tis yes, now no,
And what to say, O wretched me! I know not.
And yet it is none else. With clear bright glance
Advancing she salutes me, and declares
It is mine own Ismene, no one else.

OEDIPUS: What say'st thou, daughter?

ANTIGONE: That I see thy child,
My sister; now her voice will bid thee know.

(*Enter Ismene, followed by an attendant.*)

ISMENE: O dearest one. My father and my sister!
Of all names sweetest. Hard it was to find,
And now for sorrow it is hard to see.

OEDIPUS: Art thou then come?

ISMENE: Not easy was the way.

OEDIPUS: Touch me, my child.

ISMENE: I touch you both at once.

OEDIPUS: Hast thou appeared?

ISMENE: O father, sad, most sad!

OEDIPUS: O child, dear child!

ISMENE: O lives of two-fold woe!

OEDIPUS: Hers and mine, mean'st thou?

ISMENE: Yea, and mine the third!

OEDIPUS: Why com'st thou, child?

ISMENE: In care for thee, my father!

OEDIPUS: Did'st thou then yearn . . . . ?

ISMENE: I come to tell my tale,
With the one faithful servant that I had.

OEDIPUS: Where are thy brothers, young and strong to work?

ISMENE: E'en as they are. A fearful fate is theirs.

OEDIPUS: Oh, like in all things, both in nature's bent,
And mode of life, to Egypt's evil ways,
Where men indoors sit weaving at the loom,
And wives outdoors must earn their daily bread.
Of you, my children, those who ought to toil,
Keep house at home, like maidens in their prime,
And ye, in their stead, wear yourselves to death,
For me and for my sorrows. She, since first
Her childhood's nurture ceased, and she grew strong,
Still wandering with me sadly evermore,
Leads the old man through many a wild wood's paths,
Hungry and footsore, threading on her way.

And many a storm and many a scorching sun
Bravely she bears, and little recks of home,
So that her father find his daily bread.
And thou, my child, before did'st come to me
All oracles to tell me (those Cadmeians
Not knowing of thy errand) which were given
Touching this feeble frame; and thou wast still
A faithful guardian, when from out the land
They drove me. And what tidings bring'st thou now,
Ismene, to thy father? What has led
Thy steps from home? for that thou com'st not idly,
Nor without cause for fear, I know full well.

ISMENE: The sufferings which I suffered, O my father,
Tracking thy life where thou may'st chance to dwell,
This I pass over, for I like not twice
To grieve my soul, first bearing pain itself,
And then relating. But I come to tell
The ills that now thy wretched sons befall:
Till now they were content to leave the throne
To Creon, nor defile their country's fame,
Bearing in mind the ancient taint of blood
Which cleaves to all thy miserable house:
But now, an evil spirit from the Gods,
And their own mood of hate, have seized on them,
Thrice miserable, to grasp at sovereignty
And regal sway. And he, the youngest born,
His elder brother Polyneices robs
Of kingly throne, and drives him from the land.
And he, (for so reports come thick and fast,)
An exile goes to Argos in the dale,
There forms new ties, and gains a friendly host
Of warriors round him, as if Argos meant,
Or to bring low the plain of Cadmus old
In conquest, or exalt its fame to heaven.

These are no words, my father, no vain show,
But fearful deeds. And I as yet know not
What way the pity of the Gods will work.

OEDIPUS:
And had'st thou any hope the Gods would look
On me with pity, and deliverance give?

ISMENE:
To me, at least, these oracles give hope.

OEDIPUS:
What oracles? And what has been revealed?

ISMENE:
That the men there should seek to bring thee back,
Or dead or living, if they wish for safety.

OEDIPUS:
And who from such as I could safety gain?

ISMENE:
They say that all their power depends on thee.

OEDIPUS:
Am I a hero then, as good as dead?

ISMENE:
The Gods did vex thee once, they prosper now.

OEDIPUS:
'Tis vain to prosper in his age a man
In youth low fallen.

ISMENE:
                          Know that Creon comes
On this account, ere many days be past.

OEDIPUS:
With what intent, my daughter? Make this clear.

ISMENE:
That they may place thee near Cadmeian ground,
And keep thee, but the borders of the land
Thou must not enter.

OEDIPUS:
                          And what help will come
From this my presence lying at their door?

ISMENE:
Thy grave dishonoured brings disgrace on them.

OEDIPUS:
This one might know, without the voice of God.

ISMENE:
On this account they wish to have thee near
Their country, not where thou may'st roam at will.

OEDIPUS: And will they cover me with Theban dust?

ISMENE: Thy father's blood makes that impossible.

OEDIPUS: Then never shall they have me in their power!

ISMENE: Great sorrow to the Thebans will this bring.

OEDIPUS: What chance or change shall bring that end to pass?

ISMENE: Thy wrath, when they shall gather round thy tomb.

OEDIPUS: From whom heard'st thou, my child, the things thou
tell'st?

ISMENE: From men who went to seek the Delphic shrine.

OEDIPUS: Has Phoebus then declared these things of us?

ISMENE: So said the men who thence returned to Thebes.

OEDIPUS: Did either of my sons hear this report?

ISMENE: Both heard alike, and knew its gist right well.

OEDIPUS: And did those vile ones, knowing this, prefer
The pride of power to all their love for me?

ISMENE: 'Tis pain to hear such words, . . . and yet I bear them.

OEDIPUS: O that the Gods might never lull to rest
The destined strife between them, and would grant
To me the end of all the deadly war
For which they lift the spear! Then neither he
Who holds the sceptre and the throne should stay,
Nor he who now has left the city's gates
Return in peace. Lo! they would none of me,
Their father that begat them, helped me not,
Thus poor, dishonoured, exiled; but by them
I was sent forth an outlawed fugitive.
But thou wilt say, it may be, at my wish
My country rightly gave this boon to me.

Not so, not so, for on that self-same day,
When yet my thoughts were hot, and all my wish,
My one desire, to perish, stoned to death,
No man came forward then to help that wish;
But later, when the sorrow had grown slack,
And I perceived my passion had outstripped
My former faults with lavish punishment,
Then did our state, for its part, drive me forth
Full late to exile. And my sons that might
Have helped their father, would not stir to act;
And I, for lack of one small word, went roaming,
A beggar and a fugitive. And these,
Girls as they are, with such strength as they have,
Give me my daily food; from them I gain
Rest without fear, and every kindly help.
But those two brothers chose, instead of me
Their father, kingly thrones and sceptred sway,
To play their parts as sovereigns in the land.
But never shall they make me their ally,
Nor from their rule o'er Thebes shall aught of good
For ever come. This know I, hearing both
The oracles she brings, and thinking o'er
Those older words that Phoebus brought on me.
Wherefore to seek me let them Creon send,
Or any man whose power the country owns.
For if ye will but stand, my friends, on guard,
With these thrice awful, dread Protectresses,
Then for your country's welfare ye shall gain
A great Deliverer, trouble to its foes.

CHORUS: Worthy of pity art thou, Oedipus;
Both thou and these thy daughters. But as thou
Dost of this land proclaim thyself the saviour,
I wish to give thee counsel for thy good.

OEDIPUS: Help me, true friend, as willing to do all.

CHORUS: Make thine atonement to these Powers, to whom
           Thou camest first, profaning this their soil.

OEDIPUS: After what fashion? Tell me, O my friends.

CHORUS: First, offer from the ever-flowing stream
           Libations sacred, lifting holy hands.

OEDIPUS: And when I take this pure and stainless stream . . . ?

CHORUS: Vases there are, the work of skilful hands;
           Crown thou their rims and handles at the mouth.

OEDIPUS: With fresh green boughs, or locks of wool, or how?

CHORUS: Around them twine a young lamb's snow-white locks.

OEDIPUS: So be it. And what then remains to do?

CHORUS: Then pour libations turning to the East.

OEDIPUS: And shall I pour with these same urns thou tell'st of?

CHORUS: Pour three libations, all at once the last . . .

OEDIPUS: With what shall I fill this? Instruct me here.

CHORUS: Water and honey. Wine thou must not add.

OEDIPUS: Why this, when vine-leaves shadow all the land?

CHORUS: Branches thrice nine of olive then place here,
           On either hand; then offer up these prayers.

OEDIPUS: I fain would hear them. Crown of all are they.

CHORUS: Eumenides, the Gentle Ones, we call them,
           With gentle hearts receive and save your suppliant;
           Pray, both thyself, and some one in thy stead,
           In low voice speaking, not in lengthened cry;
           Then, turning not, withdraw. If thou dost this,

> I will stand by thee boldly; else for thee,
> O stranger friend, I should be full of fear.

OEDIPUS: Hear ye, my children, what these townsmen say?

ANTIGONE: We hear. Do thou command us what is right.

OEDIPUS: I may not go. Two evils press on me,
My failing strength and loss of power to see;
Let one of you go on and do these things.
For one soul working in the strength of love
Is mightier than ten thousand to atone;
But what ye do, do quickly. Only this
I ask you, leave me not. This feeble frame,
Bereaved of you, unguided cannot creep.

ISMENE: I go to do thy bidding. But the place
Which it is mine to seek, I fain would learn.

CHORUS: Beyond this grove, O maiden. And if still
Thou lackest aught, our townsman here shall tell thee.

ISMENE: I would go forth to this. Antigone,
Guard thou our father. For a parent's sake,
Though one may toil, one should the toil forget.

(Exit Ismene.)

CHORUS: To stir the buried evil of the past,
I know, is fearful; yet I fain would ask—

OEDIPUS: Of what?

CHORUS: Of thy great sorrow, pitiful,
Grievous, perplexing, ever by thy side.

OEDIPUS: By all thy ties of kindness, gentle friend,
Bid me not open deeds of foulest shame.

CHORUS: The wide-spread rumour growing evermore,
            I fain would hear, my friend, the truth in all.

OEDIPUS: Woe! woe!

CHORUS: Be patient, I beseech thee.

OEDIPUS: Woe, woe is me!

CHORUS: Comply, as I have done with thy desire!

OEDIPUS: Full evil fortune have I borne, my friends,
            But all against my will; for these, God knows,
            Were none of them self-chosen.

CHORUS: How was this?

OEDIPUS: In shameful wedlock did my country join me
            Who nothing knew, yea, in accursèd marriage.

CHORUS: And did'st thou, as I hear, thy mother's bed
            Take as thine own, in shame ineffable?

OEDIPUS: Ah me! 'tis death to me to hear it said,
            O stranger! And these children—they were born . . .

CHORUS: What sayest thou?

OEDIPUS: Two sorrows they were born . . .

CHORUS: O Zeus!

OEDIPUS: From the same womb to which I owed my birth.

CHORUS: Are they thy daughters?

OEDIPUS: Yea, their father's sisters.

CHORUS: Ah woe!

OEDIPUS: Ah woe! ten thousand tangled ills . . .

CHORUS: Thou suffer'dst . . .

OEDIPUS:	Yes, I suffered fearful things.
CHORUS:	And thou hast done . . .
OEDIPUS:	I have not done.
CHORUS:	What then?
OEDIPUS:	I did but take as gift what I, poor wretch, Had, at my country's hands, not merited.
CHORUS:	Poor sufferer, what but that? And didst thou kill . . .?
OEDIPUS:	What say'st thou now? What wishest thou to learn?
CHORUS:	Thy father?
OEDIPUS:	Ah, thou strikest blow on blow.
CHORUS:	Did'st slay him?
OEDIPUS:	Yea, I slew him; but in this . . .
CHORUS:	What sayest thou?
OEDIPUS:	I have some plea of right.
CHORUS:	How so?
OEDIPUS:	I'll tell thee. Not with knowledge clear I smote and slew him; but I did the deed, By law, not guilty, ignorant of all.
CHORUS:	Lo, Theseus comes! great Aegeus' son, our king, At thy request, to hear thy message to him.

(*Enter Theseus.*)

THESEUS:	Hearing from many, in the years gone by, (The bloody mischief thou did'st do thine eyes,) I know thee, son of Laius, who thou art; And hearing, as I came, fresh news, discern

Yet more; for thee, thy weeds and suffering face
Declare too plainly; and, with pitying heart,
I wish to ask, unhappy Oedipus,
Why thou sitt'st here, a suppliant to my state,
And to me also,—thou, and that poor girl
Who still attends thee? Tell me; dread indeed
The suffering thou should'st tell, for me to hold
Myself aloof from it. Right well I know
That I myself was reared away from home,
As thou; and, more than most men, struggled through,
In a strange land, full many a risk of life.
So from no stranger, coming as thou com'st,
Would I draw back, or fail to help and save;
I know that I am man, and I can count
No more than thou, on what the morrow brings.

OEDIPUS: Theseus, thy noble heart, with fewest words,
Permits me too to answer thee in brief;
For who I am, and of what father born,
And from what country come,—thou hast said all;
So that nought else remains but just to say
The things I wish for, and my tale is told.

THESEUS: Tell me then straightway, that I too may know.

OEDIPUS: I come to give thee this poor feeble frame,
A sorry gift, uncomely to the sight.
But gain will come of it, that far outweighs
All outward beauty.

THESEUS: And what gain is this
Thou boastest that thou bring'st?

OEDIPUS: In course of time
Thou shalt know all, but not this present hour.

THESEUS: And when shall this, the gain thou bring'st, be clear?

OEDIPUS: When I shall die, and thou shalt bury me.

THESEUS: Thou askest life's last care; what comes between
Thou dost forget, or make of no account.

OEDIPUS: For me this goeth hand in hand with that.

THESEUS: 'Tis a small thing thou ask'st, this boon of thine.

OEDIPUS: Look to it well. Not small the conflict here.

THESEUS: Mean'st thou a conflict of thy townsmen with me?

OEDIPUS: Fain would they force me thither to return.

THESEUS: Against their will, it is not good to flee.

OEDIPUS: Nay, but they never gave me what I wished.

THESEUS: O fool, in troubles passion profits not.

OEDIPUS: Hear first, then counsel. Till then, let me be.

THESEUS: Instruct me; unadvised I would not speak.

OEDIPUS: O Theseus, I have suffered ills on ills.

THESEUS: Speak'st thou of that old sorrow of thy house?

OEDIPUS: Not so. That sorrow all th' Hellenes know.

THESEUS: What more than human woe weighs sore on thee?

OEDIPUS: Thus is it with me. I was driven away
By mine own sons; and never may I tread
My country's soil, my father's murderer.

THESEUS: Why should they fetch thee then, apart to dwell?

OEDIPUS: It is the voice of God constrains them to it.

THESEUS: What evil do the oracles forebode?

OEDIPUS: That they are doomed in this thy land to fall.

THESEUS: And how should strife spring up 'twixt them and me?

OEDIPUS: O son of Aegeus, unto Gods alone
Nor age can come, nor destined hour of death.
All else the almighty Ruler, Time, sweeps on.
Earth's strength shall wither, wither strength of limb,
And trust decays, and mistrust grows apace;
And the same spirit lasts not among them
That once were friends, nor joineth state with state.
To these at once, to those in after years,
Sweet things grow bitter, then turn sweet again.
And what if now at Thebes all things run smooth
And well towards thee, Time, in myriad change,
A myriad nights and days brings forth; and thus
In these, for some slight cause, they yet may spurn
In battle, all their pledge of faithfulness.
And there this body, sleeping in the grave,
All cold and stiff, shall drink warm blood of men,
If Zeus be Zeus, and His son, Phoebus, true.
But, since it is ill done to speak of things
Best left unstirred, leave me where I began,
Thine own pledge keeping faithfully, and ne'er
Shalt thou have cause to say thou took'st me in,
Me, Oedipus, a guest unprofitable
To this thy land, unless the Gods deceive me.

CHORUS: Such words, my king, and others like to them,
Long since, this man has promised to perform.

THESEUS: Who then were bold enough to cast aside
His kindly feeling for a man like this,
Who may claim, first, the ancient mutual ties
The open hearth of men allied in arms;
And next, has come a suppliant of the Gods,
And to my land and me full tribute pays?
These claims I reverence, and will not disown
My friendship for him; but will welcome him

In this our land. And if it please our guest
Here to remain, I charge thee o'er him watch;
But if to go with me shall please thee, Oedipus,
I leave it thy choice to go or stay,
As thou think'st best, myself content with that.

OEDIPUS: O Zeus! give blessings to such men as this!

THESEUS: What then desirest thou? To go with me?

OEDIPUS: If it were lawful; . . . But the place is here.

THESEUS: For what design? Speak! I will not oppose thee.

OEDIPUS: Where I shall conquer those who cast me forth.

THESEUS: That were great boon for this thy stay with us.

OEDIPUS: If what thou say'st abides with thee in act.

THESEUS: Fear not as touching me; I ne'er will fail thee.

OEDIPUS: I bind thee not, like baser men, by oaths.

THESEUS: No more by that thou 'dst gain than from my word.

OEDIPUS: How wilt thou act then?

THESEUS: What alarms thee most?

OEDIPUS: Men will come here . . . .

THESEUS: Let these take charge of them.

OEDIPUS: Beware, in leaving me . . . .

THESEUS: Nay, tell me not
What to beware.

OEDIPUS: And yet I needs must, fearing . . . .

THESEUS: Fear my heart knows not.

OEDIPUS: Thou know'st not their threats.

THESEUS: But this I know, that no man of them all
Shall drag thee off from hence against my will.
Full many men have uttered many a threat
In random wrath, but when their mind is calm,
The threatenings vanish and are seen no more.
If they, perchance, waxed fierce, and spake big words
About thy going back, yet I know well
They'll find the sea full wide and rough for them.
I bid thee, then, apart from my resolve,
Take heart, if it was Phoebus sent thee here:
And, even in my absence this I know,
My very name will guard thee from all harm.

      (*Exit Theseus.*)

      Strophe 1

CHORUS: Of all the land far famed for goodly steeds,
Thou com'st, O stranger, to the noblest spot,
      Colonus, glistening bright,
Where evermore, in thickets freshly green,
      The clear-voiced nightingale
      Still haunts, and pours her song,
      By purpling ivy hid,
And the thick leafage sacred to the God,
      With all its myriad fruits,
      By mortal's foot untouched,
      By sun's hot ray unscathed,
      Sheltered from every blast;
There wanders Dionysus evermore,
      In full, wild revelry,
And waits upon the Nymphs who nursed his youth.

Antistrophe 1

And there, beneath the gentle dews of heaven,
The fair narcissus with its clustered bells
    Blooms ever, day by day,
Of old the wreath of mightiest Goddesses;
      And crocus golden-eyed;
      And still unslumbering flow
      Cephisus' wandering streams;
They fail not from their spring, but evermore,
    Swift-rushing into birth,
    Over the plain they sweep,
    The land of broad, full breast,
    With clear and stainless wave:
Nor do the Muses in their minstrel choirs,
    Hold it in slight esteem,
Nor Aphrodite with her golden reins.

Strophe 2

And in it grows a marvel such as ne'er
    On Asia's soil I heard,
Nor the great Dorian isle from Pelops named,
    A plant self-sown, that knows
    No touch of withering age,
    Terror of hostile swords,
    Which here on this our ground
    Its high perfection gains,
The grey-green foliage of the olive-tree,
    Rearing a goodly race:
    And never more shall man,
    Or young, or bowed with years,
    Give forth the fierce command,
    And lay it low in dust.

For lo! the eye of Zeus,
Zeus of our olive groves,
That sees eternally,
Casteth its glance thereon,
And she, Athena, with the clear, grey eyes.

Antistrophe 2

And yet another praise is mine to sing,
    Gift of the mighty God
To this our city, mother of us all,
    Her greatest, noblest boast,
    Famed for her goodly steeds,
    Famed for her bounding colts,
    Famed for her sparkling sea.
Poseidon, son of Cronus, Lord and King,
    To Thee this boast we owe,
    For first in these our streets
    Thou to the untamed horse
    Did'st use the conquering bit:
    And here the well-shaped oar,
    By skilled hands deftly plied,
    Still leapeth through the sea,
    Following in wondrous guise,
The fair Nereids with their hundred feet.

ANTIGONE: O land, thus blest with praises that excel,
'Tis now thy task to prove these glories true.

(*Creon is seen approaching.*)

OEDIPUS: What new thing happens, child?

ANTIGONE: Creon comes!
And comes, my father, not without an escort.

OEDIPUS: Now, dear and honoured friends, of reverend age,
In you is my one goal of safety found.

CHORUS: Take heart! Thou 'lt find it; old although I be,
Our country's strength has not yet waxen old.

(Enter Creon, attended by guards.)

CREON: Ye worthy dwellers of this land, I see,
Your faces showing it, ye feel some fear
At this my sudden entry. Yet, I pray you,
Shrink ye not from me, speak no evil words,
For I am come with no design to act,
Seeing I too am old, and know that I
Come to a city, great and powerful,
As any is in Hellas. I was sent,
Old as I am, this old man to persuade
To follow me to yon Cadmeian plain,
Not one man's envoy, but by all sent forth,
Because by kinship it is mine to mourn,
More than all others, this man's sufferings.
And thou, O woe-worn Oedipus, list to me,
And homeward turn. The whole Cadmeian race
Invites thee heartily, I, most of all,
Since most, unless I were of all men basest,
I mourn, old man, for all thy many woes,
Beholding thee in all thy misery,
A stranger, and a wanderer evermore,
And wanting still the very means of life.
With one attendant, who, I never thought,
Would come to such a depth of ignominy,
As she, poor girl, has fallen to, who still,
Caring for thee, and that poor face of thine,
In beggar's guise lives on,—at her age too,
Unsought in marriage, to the lust exposed

98

Of any passing stranger. Woe is me!
Is it not foul reproach of which I spake,
Reproaching thee, and me, and all thy race?
Yet, since 'tis vain to hide what all men see,
Do thou, by all my country's Gods, give ear,
And list to me, O Oedipus, and hide them,
As thou can'st do, if willing to return
To thine own city, and thy father's house,
To this state here a kindly farewell giving,
For it is worthy. But thine own that nursed
Thee long ago may claim yet more regard.

OEDIPUS: O shameless one, all daring! weaving still
Some crafty scheme from every righteous word,
Why triest thou again, and fain would'st take
Me prisoner, where I most should grieve to be?
For long ago, when I was mad with woe,
And I had joyed to leave the land for aye,
Thou would'st not grant this boon to me who asked;
But when my wrath was sated, saner grown,
And it was pleasant to abide at home,
Then did'st thou thrust me, drive me out by force,
And kinship then had little weight with thee.
And now again, when thou dost see this state
Is friendly to me, it, and all its race,
Thou fain would'st drag me off, with glozing words
Hard purpose masking. But what profits it
To show thy love to men against their will?
Just as if one, when thou did'st seek and beg,
Should give thee nought, nor even wish to help.
And when thy soul was filled with all thy wish,
Should give, when favour little favour wins.
Would'st thou not find this boon an empty show?
Yet such the thing that thou dost offer me,
Goodly in show, yet mischievous in act.

These too I'll tell, that I may show thee base;
Thou com'st to take me, not to take me home,
But on the borders of thy land to place me,
That so thy state from troubles may be freed,
Untouched by any evil from this land.
That shall not be; but this shall be thy lot,
My stern Avenger dwelling with thee still;
And those my sons shall gain of that my land
Enough to die in, that and nothing more.
Do not I wiser prove for Thebes than thou?
Yea, far, as I more clearly hear the voice
Of Phoebus, and of Zeus who calls Him son?
But here thy mouth has come with feignèd lips,
Speaking thy pointed words. Yet thou may'st reap
In this thy speech more evil far than good.
But since I know I move thee not, depart,
And leave us here in peace, for we should fare,
E'en as we are, not badly, being content.

CREON: Think'st thou I prosper less in what concerns thee,
Than thou in what concerns thyself, in this?

OEDIPUS: I am content, if thou dost not prevail,
Persuading me, or these my neighbours here.

CREON: O man ill-starred! shall time not make thee wise?
Wilt thou still bring to age such foul disgrace?

OEDIPUS: Thy gift of speech is wondrous; but I know
None pleading well all causes, and yet just.

CREON: Much speech is one thing, well-timed speech another.

OEDIPUS: Thy speech, of course, is brief and well-timed too.

CREON: Not so, to one whose wisdom is as thine.

OEDIPUS: Go thou thy way, for in the name of these

I say it, watch me not with ill intent,
To plan attack where I should dwell in peace.

CREON: Not thee, but these I take as witnesses
What words thou giv'st thy friends; should I seize
thee . . .

OEDIPUS: And who will seize me, spite of these allies?

CREON: Yet, without this, there's grief in store for thee.

OEDIPUS: What act do these thy threatening words portend?

CREON: Of thy two daughters one but now I seized,
And sent her off; the other follows soon.

OEDIPUS: Ah me!

CREON: Full soon thou wilt have more to groan for.

OEDIPUS: Hast thou my child?

CREON: And this one too ere long.

(*Guards seize Antigone.*)

OEDIPUS: Ho! friends, what do ye? Will ye thus betray me,
Nor drive this godless monster from your land?

CHORUS: Depart, O stranger, quickly! Wrong the deed
Thou doest now; wrong what thou did'st before.

CREON: (*To his guards.*) Now is your time, against her will to
seize her,
If with her own free will she goeth not.

ANTIGONE: Ah, wretched me! And whither shall I fly?
What help from Gods or mortals shall I find?

CHORUS: What means this, stranger?

CREON: Him I will not touch,
But this girl's mine.

OEDIPUS: O rulers of the land!

CHORUS: Not just, O stranger, are the deeds thou doest.

CREON: Nay, just are they.

CHORUS: How can'st thou call them just?

CREON: I carry off mine own.

OEDIPUS: Ho! city! to the rescue!

CHORUS: What means this, stranger? Wilt not let her go?
Soon thou wilt force me to the test of strength.

(The Chorus try to rescue Antigone.)

CREON: Keep off, I tell thee.

CHORUS: Not while thou attempt'st
Such things as these.

CREON: If thou dost injure me,
Thou with my state wilt have to wage thy war.

OEDIPUS: Did not I tell thee this?

CHORUS: Let go thy hand
From off this maid!

CREON: Command not where thou 'rt weak.

CHORUS: *(To one of Creon's troops.)* I bid thee set her free.

CREON: *(To the same.)*   I bid thee go!

CHORUS: Come, neighbours, come! Come hither to our help:
Our state is injured, yes, our state. With might
Come hither, help!

ANTIGONE: Ah, friends! ah, friends! they drag me, wretched one!

OEDIPUS: Where art thou, child?

ANTIGONE: Against my will I go.

OEDIPUS: Stretch forth thine hands, my child.

ANTIGONE: No power have I.

CREON: (*To the guards.*) Will ye not lead her?

OEDIPUS: Woe is me! all woe.

  (*Guards carry off Antigone.*)

CREON: No longer, then, on these props leaning, thou
  Shalt travel onward. But since thou wilt thwart
  Thy country and thy friends, at whose behest
  I do these deeds, although myself a king,
  Thwart us, if so it please thee. For, in time,
  I know right well, thou 'lt learn to see thyself
  As neither now consulting thine own good,
  Nor in the time that's past, when thou did'st act
  Against the counsel of thy friends, and yield
  To that fierce wrath that plagues thee ceaselessly.

  (*Moves as if about to depart.*)

CHORUS: Hold there, my friend!

  (*Advances towards Creon.*)

CREON: I tell thee, touch me not.

CHORUS: Though robbed of these, I will not let thee go.

CREON: Thou 'lt make thy state a larger ransom pay,

For not on these alone I lay my hand.

CHORUS: What mean'st thou then?

CREON: Him also will I take!

CHORUS: Thy words are big.

CREON: Yet it shall soon be done,
Unless the ruler of this land forbid me.

OEDIPUS: O shameful threat! Shalt thou lay hands on me?

CREON: Silence, I charge thee!

OEDIPUS: May these Goddess-Powers
Not smite me speechless till I speak my curse
On thee, thou vile one, robbing me by force
Of that last light, when other lights were quenched.
For this may yon bright Sun-god, scanning all,
Grant thee thyself, and all thy race with thee,
To wear thy life in dreary age like mine.

CREON: See ye these things, ye dwellers in this land?

OEDIPUS: They see both me and thee, and judge that I,
Wronged by thy deeds, by words defend myself.

CREON: I'll check my wrath no more. Although alone.
And worn with age, I'll lead him hence by force.

OEDIPUS: Ah, wretched me!

CHORUS: Thy pride is great, my friend,
If that thou thinkest thus to work thy will.

CREON: And yet I think it.

CHORUS: Then our country's lost.

CREON: In a just cause the weak o'erpowers the strong.

OEDIPUS: Hear ye what things he utters?

CHORUS: Things which he
Shall ne'er accomplish!

CREON: Zeus knows that, not thou!

CHORUS: And is not this an outrage?

CREON: Outrage! aye;
Still thou must bear it!

CHORUS: Ho! ye people, come!
Ye rulers of this land come quickly—haste!
These men are getting far upon their way.

(Enter Theseus, followed by Athenians.)

THESEUS: What means this cry? What do ye? What ill fearing
Have ye thus stopped me in the act of slaughter,
Even at the altar, to the God of Ocean,
Guardian of this Colonus? Tell your tale out,
That I may know why I have rushed in haste thus,
With greater speed than one would walk for pleasure.

OEDIPUS: O dearest friend!—for well I know thy voice—
At this man's hands I suffer fearful wrongs.

THESEUS: What are they? Who has injured thee? Speak on!

OEDIPUS: This Creon, whom thou seest, has torn from me
The only pair that I as children claim.

THESEUS: How say'st thou?

OEDIPUS: What I suffer thou hast heard.

THESEUS: Let someone, then, to yonder altars go
With utmost speed to summon all the people,
Both horse and foot, to hasten, tarrying not
For sacrifice, with loosened rein, and meet
Where the two paths of travellers converge,

Lest those two maidens slip from out our hands,
And I, outdone, become a laughing-stock
To him, this stranger. Go, I bid you, quickly.
And as for him, if I were wroth with him,
E'en as he merits, he should not depart
Unhurt from me; but with the self-same laws
With which he came shall he be recompensed,
Those and no others. (*To Creon.*) Never shalt thou stir
From out this land until before mine eyes
Thou place those maidens. Thou dost grievous wrong
To thine own self, thy fathers, and thy country,
Who, coming to a state that loves the right,
And without law does nothing, sett'st at nought
The things it most reveres, and rushing in,
Tak'st what thou wilt, with deeds of violence.
Thou must have deemed my city void of men,
Slave-like, submissive, and myself as nought.
And yet it was not Thebes that made thee base:
'Tis not her wont to rear unrighteous men;
Nor would'st thou win her praise, if she should hear
Thou tramplest on my rights, defiest Gods,
And rudely seizest these poor suppliants.
I truly, had I entered on thy land,
Although my cause were justest of the just,
Would not, without the ruler of the land,
Be he who may, have seized or led away;
But should have known what way I ought to live,
A stranger sojourning with citizens.
But thou dost shame a city which deserves
A better fate,—thine own; and time's full course,
Making thee old, has robbed thee of thy mind.
I told thee this before, and tell thee now,
To bring the girls as quickly as thou can'st,
Unless thou fain would'st live an alien here,

By force, against thy will. And this I say,
With all my soul, as well as with my tongue.

CHORUS: See'st thou, O stranger, how the case doth stand?
Just by thy birth and fame, thy deeds are wrong.

CREON: Not that I count this city void of men,
(I use thy words, O son of Aegeus old,)
Nor void of counsel, have I done this deed,
Well knowing that no zeal for those my kindred
Would ever lead it to receive them here
In spite of my commands. I also knew
Ye ne'er would shield a parricide impure,
Nor one whose marriage was an incest foul;
I knew that in this land a Council met
Upon the hill of Ares, wise and good,
Which suffers not such wanderers to dwell
Within their city. Trusting this report,
I ventured on this seizure. Yet e'en thus
I had not done it, but he heaped his curse
On me and on my house, and, suffering thus,
I claimed the right of rendering ill for ill,
(For headstrong wrath knows no old age but death;
The dead are callous to the touch of pain.)
Wherefore do what thou wilt, for though I speak
With justice on my side, yet, being alone,
But little power is left me. Yet thy deeds
Old as I am I'll strive to render back.

OEDIPUS: O shameless soul! on which, think'st thou, thy scorn
Will fall most heavily, my age or thine?
Who with thy lips dost tell the goodly tale,
Of murders, incest, sad calamities,
Which I, poor wretch, against my will endured;
For thus it pleased the Gods, incensed, perhaps,
Against my father's house for guilt of old.

For, as regards my life, thou could'st not find
One spot of guilt, in recompense for which
I sinned these sins against myself and mine.
Tell me, I pray, if God-sent oracles
Declared his son's hand should my father slay,
How could'st thou justly heap reproach on me,
Who had no nurture at my father's hands,
Nor at my mother's, but, as one self-grown,
Rose then to manhood? Or, if once again,
Born, as I was, to misery and shame,
I with my father came to blows, and slew him,
Not knowing what I did, or unto whom;
How can'st thou rightly blame th' unconscious sin?
And thou, all shameless, blushest not to force
My lips to speak of marriage with my mother,
With her who was thy sister. I will speak
Of these things quickly, will not hold my peace,
Since thou hast ventured on such hateful speech.
She bore me; yes, she bore me—(woe is me!)
Unknowing, bearing me who knew her not;
And having borne, to me she issue gave,
Her shame and her reproach. But this I know,
That thou of thy free will speak'st foulest words
Against her name and mine, while I, against
My will espoused her, and against my will
Now speak these things. And yet my name shall bear
No evil brand by reason of that marriage,
Nor for my father's death that thou still harp'st on,
With bitter words of shame reproaching me.
Just answer then this question that I ask:
If one should seek to slay thee here and now,
Thee, the famed just one, would'st thou stay to ask
If 'twere thy father's hand that aimed the blow,
Or would'st thou straightway parry it? I think,

As thou lov'st life, thou would'st requite thy foe,
And would'st not look so narrowly at right;
Such ills, at any rate, were those I fell on,
The Gods still leading me; nor can I think
My father's soul, if it returned to life,
Would plead against me here. But thou think'st fit,—
Since just thou 'rt not, as one who deems it right
To speak of all things, whether fit for speech
Or things which none may utter,—before these
To heap reproach on me. And Theseus' name
It suits thee well to flatter, and to speak
Of Athens, and her goodly polity;
And yet thus praising, thou forgettest this,
That she, if any land reveres the Gods,
In this excels; and yet from her thou dar'st
To steal a suppliant, grey and hoar with age,
And those two maidens hast already taken.
And for these deeds, these Goddess-Powers I call
And supplicate, and weary with my prayers,
To come as helpers and allies, that thou
May'st learn their mettle who this land defend.

CHORUS: The man, O King, speaks nobly, and his woes
Are grievous, and they call us to assist him.

THESEUS: Enough of words, for they who snatched their prey
Haste on, while we who suffer wrong stand still.

CREON: What orders giv'st thou to a man defenceless?

THESEUS: That thou should'st lead the way, and I should go
Thy escort, so that if thou hast his girls
Within our borders, thou may'st show them me;
But if they get beyond, we need not toil;
For there are others, hastening to pursue,
And those who flee shall never thank the Gods

As 'scaped from this our land: but lead thou on,
And know that thou who hold'st thy prey art held,
And chance has caught thee, hunter as thou art;
For gains, ill gotten by a fraud unjust,
Can never prosper. And another's help
Thou shalt not have in this, for well I know
Thou had'st not ventured on so great a wrong
Alone, unbacked, but there is some one else,
Trusting to whom thou did'st it. And for me,
I must look well to this: nor leave my state
By one man conquered, weak and powerless.
Regard'st thou aught of this, or seems it vain,
Both now, and when thou planned'st these thy schemes?

CREON: While thou speak'st here, I fault with nothing find;
           When we reach home, we shall know what to do.

THESEUS: Go on and threaten. Thou, O Oedipus,
           Stay here in peace and comfort, trusting me
           That I, unless I die, will never rest,
           Before I give thy children to thy hands.

OEDIPUS: God bless thee, Theseus, for thy noble heart,
           And all thy just and generous care for us.

           (*Exeunt Theseus and Athenians, with Creon and his
           guards.*)

           Strophe 1

CHORUS: Ah! would that I were there
                Where onset fierce of men
                Arrayed for fight shall join
                In brazen-throated war;
                Or at the Pythian fane,
                Or by the torch-lit shores,

Where awful Powers still watch,
O'er solemn rites for men of mortal race;
Whose golden key is set upon the lips
Of priests, Eumolpidae, who tend their shrine.
        There, so I deem, will meet
        Our Theseus, brave in fight,
        And those two sisters, proof
        Against all toil and pain,
        Will meet on this our land,
With cry, that uttereth all their hearts' desire.

Antistrophe 1

        Or else, perchance, they cross
        The side that westward slopes
        Of yonder snow-crowned height,
        On to Oeatis' lawns,
        Speeding on goodly steeds,
        Or race of chariots swift;
        Yes, they will take their prey,
For terrible our townsmen's strength for war,
And terrible the might of Theseus's sons.
For every horse's curb is gleaming bright,
        And all that sit their steeds
        Rush forth with loosened reins,
        Who at Athena's shrine,
        Where on her steed she sits,
        Bow down, or homage pay
To Rhea's son, the sea-God, ruling earth.

Strophe 2

Strike they or do they linger? Shadowy hopes
        Come on my soul, that he

Perchance surrenders now
The maiden who hath borne
Full many a grief, and many a wrong endured
At her own kinsmen's hands.
Yes, Zeus this day will work, will work His way;
Prophet of brave deeds I.
Ah would that I, a dove on pinions swift,
Might gain some cloud that floats in aether clear,
And glad my longing eyes
With sight of this fierce conflict of the brave.

Antistrophe 2

O Zeus! thou Lord omnipotent of Gods,
Who all on earth beholdest,
Grant that our country's chiefs,
With strength for victory,
May lay their ambush, and may seize their prey;
And thou, O child of Zeus,
Pallas, Athena; thou too huntsman-God,
Apollo, in thy strength,
And she, thy sister, following evermore
Swift-footed antelopes with dappled skin;
I pray you come and help
Doubly, this land, and its inhabitants.

(*Theseus is seen approaching with Antigone and Ismene.*)

CHORUS: O way-worn stranger, thou wilt not reproach
Thy watchman as false prophet, for I see
These maidens now approaching us once more.

OEDIPUS: Where? where? How say'st thou?

ANTIGONE: (*Rushing to Oedipus.*) My father, O my father!
Oh! that some God would grant thee but to see
This best of men who brings us back to thee.

OEDIPUS: Are you both here, my child?

ANTIGONE: Yes, Theseus' hands
And those of his dear comrades rescued us.

OEDIPUS: My child, draw near thy father, give to me
To clasp the form I little hoped would come.

ANTIGONE: Thou shalt have what thou ask'st. That boon thou
seek'st
Is what we yearn for.

OEDIPUS: Where then, where are ye?

ANTIGONE: Together, close to thee.

OEDIPUS: O dearest offspring!

ANTIGONE: Dear to a father is each child of his.

OEDIPUS: Props of my age are ye!

ANTIGONE: Sad age, sad props.

OEDIPUS: I have you then, ye dear ones, nor would death
Be wholly dreary, ye twain standing near.
Support me, then, on this side and on that,
Close clinging to your father. Rest awhile
From all the sad lone wanderings of the past,
And tell me briefly how the deed was done:
For at your age the fewest words are best.

ANTIGONE: Here is the man who saved us; hear thou him,
Whose is the deed, and then my task is light.

OEDIPUS: (*To Theseus.*) Oh, wonder not, my friend, if I prolong
My tedious speech, now these, beyond my hopes,

Appear again; for well I know this joy
To me has come from no one else but thee;
For thou hast saved them, thou, and only thou;
And may the Gods grant all that I could wish
To thee and to thy land. For I have found
Here only among men the fear of God,
The mood of kindness, and the truthful word;
And knowing this, I pay it back with thanks;
For what I have, I have through thee alone.
And now, O prince, I pray, thy right hand give,
That I may grasp it, and, if that may be,
Kiss thy dear brow. And yet, how dare I ask?
Why should I wish, all foul and miserable,
To touch a man upon whose soul there dwells
No taint of evil? No! I will not ask,
I will not let thee do it. They alone
Can feel for mourners who themselves have mourned.
Farewell, then, where thou art; from henceforth care
For me as well as thou hast cared to-day.

THESEUS: Not though thy words were lengthened out yet more,
For joy of these thy daughters, should I marvel,
Nor if their words thou should'st prefer to mine.
(No pain or grievance touches me in this;)
For it is still my care to make my life,
Not by my words illustrious, but by deeds.
And thus I prove it: of the things I swore
In nothing have I failed; these girls I bring
Alive, unscathed by all the threatened harm.
And how the fight was won what need to boast
All idly, when their lips shall tell thee all?
But for the news that met me as I came,
Just now, take counsel. Short enough to tell.
It yet is passing strange. And one should learn,
Being man, to think no scorn of aught that is.

114

OEDIPUS: What is this, son of Aegeus? Speak, I pray;
For I know nothing of the things thou ask'st.

THESEUS: They say that someone near of kin to thee,
Yet not from Thebes, thy city, suppliant sits
Close by Poseidon's altar, where it chanced,
When summoned here, I offered sacrifice.

OEDIPUS: What kind of man was he? and seeking what
By this his suppliant posture?

THESEUS: Nought I know
But this; he asks, they tell me, short discourse
With thee, no heavy burden.

OEDIPUS: What is this?
Of no light import is this suppliant's prayer.

THESEUS: They say he asks to come and speak with thee,
And then return in safety as he came.

OEDIPUS: Who can it be that asks a boon like this?

THESEUS: Think if at Argos any kinsman dwells
Who might desire to gain this boon from thee.

OEDIPUS: Stop, dearest friend, I pray.

THESEUS: What aileth thee?

OEDIPUS: Ask it not of me!

THESEUS: Ask not what? Say on.

OEDIPUS: I know too well, from what these girls have told me,
Who this strange suppliant is.

THESEUS: And who is he,
That I should charge the man with any fault?

OEDIPUS: My son, O prince, from whom of all that live,
I could least bear to hear the sound of speech.

THESEUS:
Why so? Hast thou not power to hear, nor do
The things thou would'st not? Why should hearing pain
  thee?

OEDIPUS:
That voice is hateful to a father's ear;
I pray thee, prince, constrain me not to yield.

THESEUS:
But if his rights as suppliant should constrain us,
Take heed that thou shew reverence for our God.

ANTIGONE:
My father, be persuaded, though I speak
But a girl's counsel. Suffer thou this friend,
E'en as he wills, to do as conscience prompts,
And as his God demands. And grant to us
That this our brother come; for, take good heart,
He shall not draw thee on against thy judgment
With words which are not fitting. What the harm
To list to words? Yea, evil deeds and plots
By words disclose themselves. He is thy child;
And therefore, O my father, 'tis not right,
Although his deeds to thee be basest, vilest,
To render ill for ill. But let him come;
Others ere now have thankless offspring reared,
And bitter wrath have felt; but they, with spells
Of friends' good counsel, charmed their souls to peace.
Look not upon the present but the past,
Thy father's and thy mother's woes, and thou,
I know full well, wilt see that evil mood
An evil issue finds for evermore;
For strong the proofs thou hast within thyself,
In those poor sightless eyeballs. Nay, but yield—
Yield thou to us. It is not good to meet
With stiff denials those who ask for right;
Nor, having met with good at others' hands,
To fail in rendering good for good received.

OEDIPUS: Your words prevail, my child, and yet your joy
To me is grievous. Be it as you will:
Only, my friend, if he should hither come,
Let no one get the mastery of my life.

THESEUS: I wish to hear those words but once, old friend,
Not twice renewed. I am not wont to boast;
But know thou'rt safe, if any God saves me.

(*Exit Theseus.*)

Strophe

CHORUS: He who seeks length of life,
Slighting the middle path,
Shall seem, to me at least,
As brooding o'er vain dreams.
Still the long days have brought
Griefs near, and nearer yet.
And joys—thou canst not see
One trace of what they were;
When a man passeth on.
To length of days beyond the rightful bourne;
But lo, the helper comes that comes to all,
When doom of Hades looms upon his sight,
The bridegroom's joy all gone,
The lyre all silent now,
The choral music hushed,
Death comes at last.

Antistrophe

Happiest beyond compare
Never to taste of life;
Happiest in order next,

Being born, with quickest speed
Thither again to turn
From whence we came.
When youth hath passed away,
With all its follies light,
What sorrow is not there?
What trouble then is absent from our lot?
Murders, strifes, wars, and wrath, and jealousy,
And, closing life's long course, the last and worst.
An age of weak caprice,
Friendless, and hard of speech,
Where, met in union strange,
Dwell ills on ills.

Epode

And here this woe-worn one
(Not I alone) is found;
As some far northern shore,
Smitten by ceaseless waves,
Is lashed by every wind;
So ever-haunting woes,
Surging in billows fierce,
Lash him from crown to base;
Some from the westering sun,
Some from the eastern dawn,
These, from the noontide south,
Those, from the midnight of Rhipaean hills.

ANTIGONE: And here, my father, so it seems, he comes,
The stranger, all alone, and, as he walks,
He sheds a flood of tears incessantly.

OEDIPUS: Who is this man?

ANTIGONE: He, who this long time past
We thought and spoke of, Polyneices, comes.

(*Enter Polyneices.*)

POLYNEICES: What shall I do, ah me! . . . mine ills bewail,
My sisters, or shed tears for what I see
My aged father suffering? I have found
Both him and you in strange land wandering;
And this his garb, whose time-worn squalidness
Matches the time-worn face, and makes the form
All foul to look on, and his uncombed hair,
Tossed by the breeze, falls o'er his sightless brow.
And she, my sister, as it seems, provides
For this poor life its daily sustenance.
All this I learn too late, me miserable!
And now, I bear my witness that I come,
As to thy keeping, basest of the base:
Learn not my faults from others. But since there,
Sharing the throne of Zeus, Compassion dwells,
Regarding all our deeds; so let it come
And dwell with thee, my father. For our faults
We shall find healing, more we cannot add.
Why art thou silent?—Speak, my father, speak;
Turn not away.—And wilt thou answer nought,
But send'st me back dishonoured?—Voiceless still?
Not speaking e'en the matter of thy wrath!
And ye, his children, ye, my sisters, strive
To ope your father's sealed and stubborn lips
That he reject me not, thus scorned and shamed,
(God's suppliant too) not one word answering.

ANTIGONE: Say, thou thyself, poor sufferer, what thou need'st,
For many words, or giving sense of joy,
Or stirring anger, or the touch of pity,
Have from the speechless drawn forth speech at last.

POLYNEICES: Well, I will tell thee. Thou dost guide me well;
First, calling on the God to give me help,

Bowed at whose shrine, the ruler of this land
Raised me, and brought me hither, granting me
To speak and hear, and safely to depart:
And this I wish, my friends, from you to gain,
And from my sisters, and my father here.
And why I came, my father, now I'll tell thee.
Behold me exiled from my fatherland,
Driven forth, because I claimed by right of age
To sit upon thy throne of sovereignty.
And so Eteocles, though younger born,
Hath thrust me forth, not baffling me in speech,
Nor coming to the test of strength and deed,
But winning o'er the state. Of this, I say,
Thy dread Erinnyes is the chiefest cause;
And next, I hear thus much by prophets told:
For when I came to Argos, Dorian named,
Making the daughter of Adrastus mine,
I gathered as confederates in my cause,
All who are chiefest in the Apian land,
Renowned in battle, that this armament,
With seven great chiefs, might follow me to Thebes,
And I might either die a noble death,
Or drive to exile those who did me wrong.
Well then, what chance has brought me hitherward?
This, O my father. With a suppliant's prayers
Both for myself, and my allies, I come,
The seven great armies by seven captains led,
That gird the plain of Thebes. And first, there comes
Amphiaraus, wielding mighty spear,
Supreme in war, supreme in auguries;
Then next in order, the Aetolian son
Of Oeneus, Tydeus named; and Argive born,
Eteoclus the third; Hippomedon,
By Talaus sent, the fourth; and Capaneus

The fifth, boasts loud that he with fiery blaze,
Will soon lay waste the citadel of Thebes,
And utterly destroy it. Sixth, there comes
Parthenopaeus, the Arcadian, named
From his chaste mother, true and worthy son
Of Atalanta. And I, last, thy son,
Or if not thine, the child of evil Fate,
Yet known as thine, I lead the Argive host
Undaunted, against Thebes. And all of us,
By these thy children, and thy life, my father,
With one accord entreat thee, and implore
To let thy mood of wrath give way to him
Who stands before thee, hastening to chastise
The brother who deprived me of my home,
And robbed me of my country. This we ask,
For if there be aught true in oracles,
They say the side thou cleavest to will win;
Wherefore, by all the fountains of thy home,
And all thy household Gods, I pray thee yield.
Poor and in exile we, in exile thou,
And thou and I, the same ill fortune sharing,
Live, hangers-on on others, while, alas!
The despot lord at home, in pride of state
Mocks at us both; but I, if thou wilt join
Thy mind with mine, will scatter all his might,
Without much waste of trouble or of time,
And so will bring thee to thy home once more,
Stablish myself, and cast him out by force.
And this, if thou consent, 'tis mine to boast:
Without thee I've no strength to save myself.

CHORUS: For his sake, Oedipus, who sent him here,
Send the man back, with answer as seems fit.

OEDIPUS: Were it not so, my friends, that he who rules

This land had sent him, Theseus, asking me
To let him hear my words, no voice of mine
His ears had heard. But now he shall go forth
Gaining his end, and hearing words from me
Which never shall bring gladness to his life.
For thou, thou vile one, having in thy hands
The thrones and sceptre which thy brother has,
Who rules in Thebes, did'st drive thy father forth,
And mad'st him homeless, wearing weeds like these,
Which now thou weep'st to look on, when in grief
Like mine thou too art fallen. These are things
I may not weep for: I must bear them still,
While life lasts, counting thee my murderer;
For thou wast he who plunged me in this woe;
Thou drov'st me into exile; by thy deed,
A wanderer through the world, I beg my bread,
And had I not these girls to care for me,
That too would fail, for aught that thou would'st do.
But now they save my life; they tend on me;
No women they, but men in will to toil:
But ye are not my sons; I own ye not.
As yet the God forbears to look on thee,
As soon He shall, if these thy armies move
Against the towers of Thebes. It may not be
That thou shalt ever lay that city waste,
But thou thyself shalt fall, with blood defiled;
And so shall fall thy brother. Once before
I breathed these curses deep upon you both,
And now I bid them come as my allies,
That ye may learn the reverence due from sons,
Nor, being what you are, think scorn of me,
Your blind old father; (these thou look'st on here
Have done far other deeds) and therefore they,
Those Curses, sway thy prayers, thy sovereignty,

If still there dwells beside the throne of Zeus
The Eternal Right that rests on oldest laws;
And thou—may ruin seize thee, loathed and base!
I am no more thy father; take my curse
Which now I pour on thee, thy native land
Never by sword to conquer, nor again
Return to Argos in the dale, but die,
Slain by a brother's hand, and slaying him
Who drove thee forth to exile. So I curse
And call on that drear dark of Tartarus,
My father's home, to snatch thee from the earth,
And call on these dread Powers, and I invoke
Ares who stirred this fearful hate in you.
Hear this, and go thy way! And then proclaim
To all the race of Cadmus, and to those
Thy true allies, that Oedipus has left
To both his sons, such legacies as these.

CHORUS: I cannot wish thee joy of thy late journey,
O Polyneices! and I bid thee turn
At once with fullest speed, thy backward way.

POLYNEICES: Woe, then, for all my wandering, all my failure.
Woe, too, for all my friends. Is this the goal
For which from Argos starting, (wretched me!)
We hither came? an end I dare not tell
To any of my friends, nor turn them back;
But needs must meet my fate without a word.
But O my sisters, ye—for ye have heard
My father's bitter curse—I charge you both,
If these dire curses find fulfilment dread,
And it is given you homeward to return,
Do not ye scorn me: give me honours meet,
A seemly burial, decent funeral rites;
And this your praise, which now ye get from him

For whom ye labour, other praise shall bear,
No whit inferior, for your love to me.

ANTIGONE: I pray thee, Polyneices, yield to me.

POLYNEICES: In what, thou dear Antigone? Speak on.

ANTIGONE: Lead back thy host to Argos, slackening not,
Nor ruin both thy country and thyself.

POLYNEICES: It may not be. How, known as coward once,
Could I again lead forth an armament?

ANTIGONE: And why, dear boy, need'st thou be wroth again?
What profit hast thou in thy country's fall?

POLYNEICES: Retreat is base; and base that I, the elder,
Should thus be mocked and flouted by my brother.

ANTIGONE: And see'st thou then, how those his oracles
Thou leadest to fulfilment, that you both
Should meet your death, each from the other's hand?

POLYNEICES: His wish begets the thought. We may not yield.

ANTIGONE: O wretched me! and who will follow thee,
Hearing the evils which his lips predict?

POLYNEICES: These idle threats we tell not. Wise in war
Is he who speaks the better, not the worse.

ANTIGONE: And is thy mind, my brother, fixed and firm?

POLYNEICES: Restrain me not. Sad counsel must I take,
For this my march, beforehand doomed to fail,
By him, my father, and the Erinnyes dread.
But you,—Zeus bless you, if to me in death
Ye grant the boon I asked for; for in life
Ye meet me not again. And now, release me.
Farewell! ye look upon my face no more.

ANTIGONE: Ah wretched me!

POLYNEICES: Bemoan thou not for me!

ANTIGONE: And who could keep from wailing, brother dear,
For thee, thus rushing on an open grave?

POLYNEICES: Well, I will die, if so I must.

ANTIGONE: Not so.
List thou to me.

POLYNEICES: Persuade me not to wrong.

ANTIGONE: Ah, misery! to be bereaved of thee!

POLYNEICES: These things depend on God, this way or that,
To be or not to be; but I for you
Will pray the Gods that ye may meet no harm,
Who, as all deem, no evil have deserved.

(*Exit Polyneices.*)

(*The sky grows dark, thunder is heard in the
distance.*)

Strophe 1

CHORUS: Freshly they come on me,
Fresh ills, and burdens grievous to be borne,
From this blind wanderer, unless, perchance,
        His destiny comes on him:
For what the Gods decree I cannot count
As done in vain. Time evermore looks on,
And sees these things, now overturning some,
And now, within a day, exalting them.
        O Zeus, the high heaven thunders!

OEDIPUS: My children, oh, that someone, present here,
Would call back Theseus, best and noblest, hither!

ANTIGONE: What is thy purpose, father, that thou call'st him?

OEDIPUS: This wingèd thunder sent from Zeus, will lead me
Straightway to Hades. Make good speed to send.

*(Peals of thunder are heard at intervals during the
remainder of the Choral Ode.)*

Antistrophe 1

CHORUS: So the loud thunder crashes,
Hurled forth from Zeus, with dread unspeakable,
And fear creeps up to every topmost hair.
I tremble in my soul:
For lo! the fire from heaven has blazed again.
What will the end be? Much I fear. In vain
It never comes, nor without issue dread.
O mighty heaven! O Zeus!

OEDIPUS: My children! now the destined end of life
Is come to him who stands here: flight is none.

ANTIGONE: How know'st thou this? What token comes to thee?

OEDIPUS: I know right well. But, oh, let someone fetch,
Losing no time, the ruler of the land!

Strophe 2

CHORUS: Ah! ah! again the crash
Rolls piercingly around.
Be pitiful, O God, be pitiful,
If thou bring'st darkness on our mother-land;
And may I find thee gracious evermore,

Nor, looking on a man accursèd, reap
    A boon that profits not.
    King Zeus, I call on thee!

OEDIPUS: Is your chief near? And will he find me, children,
    Still living, still with wonted powers of mind?

ANTIGONE: What secret would'st thou to his soul confide?

OEDIPUS: I would fain give the good I promised him,
    Some poor return for all that I received.

Antistrophe 2

CHORUS: Come, come, my son, come quick,
        Though on the valley's edge
    Thou consecrat'st the hearth for sacrifice
    To Ocean's lord, Poseidon, come thou quick;
    For lo! the stranger fain would give to thee,
    Thy city, and thy friends, just meed of thanks
        For kind acts done. Come, haste,
        Haste onward, O my King.

(*Enter Theseus.*)

THESEUS: What means this mingled din? For lo! full plain,
    My subjects' voice, and clear the stranger's too.
    Is it the thunderbolt of Zeus, or shower
    Of hail bursts on you? When Heaven sends storm like
        this,
    All wild conjectures seem most probable.

OEDIPUS: Thou com'st, O prince, to one who much desires thee,
    And 'tis a God that blest thy journey hither.

THESEUS: What new event, O son of Laius, moves thee?

OEDIPUS: My life's scale turns i' the balance. I would fain
In death be true to thee and to thy State.

THESEUS: What token that the end is near hast thou?

OEDIPUS: The Gods themselves are heralds of my doom,
Failing in nought of all the appointed signs.

THESEUS: What is't, old friend, makes these things clear to thee?

OEDIPUS: These many thunder-claps, that still roar on,
These many flashes from the unconquered Hand.

THESEUS: I trust thy word, for I perceive thy soul
Divineth many things, and none are false;
And therefore tell me, what I needs must do.

OEDIPUS: I will inform thee, son of Aegeus old,
Of things for thee and for thy city, free
From any touch of Time's consuming power:
And I myself, with none to guide my steps,
Will show the spot where I am doomed to die.
And this, I charge thee, tell to none on earth;
Nor where the grave, nor e'en the region, tell,
Whose fields enclose it. So shall he who speaks
Give greater strength to thee than many shields,
Or hireling force called in, 'gainst neighbouring lands;
And for the mystic words which none may speak,
Thyself shalt learn them, going there alone,
For I to none of these may utter them,
Nor even to my children, though I love them.
And thou, I charge thee, hide them evermore;
And when thy death-hour comes, to one alone,
Thine eldest born, disclose them: and, in turn,
Let each reveal to those that follow him.
And so thou shalt establish this thy land,
By dragon's brood unhurt. A thousand states,

Though governed well, have lightly waxed o'er-proud;
For, though the Gods see clearly, they are slow
In marking when a man, despising them,
Turns from their worship to the scorn of fools.
Far be such fate from thee, O Aegeus' son;
These things we teach thee, though thou knowest them.
And now, for still the promptings of the God
Press on me strongly, let us seek the spot,
Nor linger on in fear. My children, follow;
A new guide I for you, as ye have been
To me your father. Come ye. Touch me not;
But let me find the hallowed grave myself,
Where fate has fixed that he who speaks shall lay
His bones to rest in this fair land we tread.
Come hither,—hither,—this way. So He leads,
Hermes the guide, and She who reigns below.
O Light! to me all dark, thou once wast mine,
And now this body feels thy ray's last touch,
Now, and no more; for now I grope my way,
To hide the dwindling remnant of my life
In Hades dark. And thou, of all friends dearest,
Live happy, thou, thy country, and thy servants;
And in your great good fortune, think of me
When I am gone, and ye are prosperous still.

(*Exit Oedipus, followed, at some distance, by Theseus, Antigone, and Ismene.*)

Strophe

CHORUS: If rightly I may come with homage due
                    To Her whom none may see,
            And thee, O King of those that dwell in night,
                    Aidoneus, O Aidoneus!

I supplicate thy aid; O grant that he,
    The stranger, wend his way,
    With no long agony,
No fate of many woes, to that dark land,
    The home of all the dead,
    Still wrapt in Stygian gloom.
For so, though many woes unmerited
    Upon his life have come,
God, the All-just, shall raise him up again.

Antistrophe

Ye Goddess Powers, who in the central dark
    Dwell evermore, and thou,
Dread form of mightiest monster, who, they say,
    Still find'st thy lair by gates
That turn on well-worn hinge continually,
    And from thy cavern growl'st,
    Watchman of Hades dread:
Bid him, thou Son of Earth and Tartarus,
    Bid him, I pray, withdraw,
    Leaving an open path,
For him who travels to the fields below,
    There where the dead abide:
Thee, I invoke, the Lord of endless sleep!

(*Enter a Messenger.*)

MESSENGER: To tell my tale, in fewest words, good sirs,
I need but say that Oedipus is dead;
But what has passed, the deeds that there were done,
My tale, in short discourse, would fail to tell.

CHORUS: Is he then dead, ill-starred one?

MESSENGER: Think of him
As having closed his weary course of life.

CHORUS: How? Was it by God-given, painless death?

MESSENGER: Yea, these are things we well may wonder at;
For how he went from hence, thou knowest well,
(Thyself being present) no friend guiding him,
But he himself still lead the way for all;
And when he neared the threshold's broken slope,
With steps of bronze fast rooted in the soil,
He stopped on one of paths that intersect,
Close to the hollow urn where still are kept
The pledges true of Perithus and Theseus;
And stopping at mid distance between it,
And the Thorician rock, and hollow pear,
And the stone sepulchre, he sat him down,
And then put off his garments travel-stained,
And then he called his girls, and bade them fetch
Clear water from the stream, and bring to him
For cleansing and libation. And they went,
Both of them, to yon hill we look upon,
Owned by Demeter of the fair green corn,
And quickly did his bidding, bathed his limbs,
And clothed him in the garment that is meet.
And when he had his will in all they did,
And not one wish continued unfulfilled,
Zeus from the dark depths thundered, and the girls
Heard it, and shuddering, at their father's knees
Falling they wept: nor did they then forbear
Smiting their breasts, nor groanings lengthened out;
And when he heard their bitter cry, forthwith
Folding his arms around them, thus he spake:
"My children! on this day ye cease to have
A father. All my days are spent and gone;

And ye no more shall lead your wretched life,
Caring for me. Hard was it, that I know,
My children! yet one word is strong to loose,
Although alone, the burden of these toils,
For love in larger store ye could not have
From any than from him who standeth here,
Of whom bereaved ye now shall live your life."
So intertwined, all wept and sobbed: and when
They ended all their wailing, and the cry
No longer rose, there came a silence. Then
A voice from someone cried aloud to him,
And filled them all with fear, that made each hair
To stand on end. For, many a time, the God
From many a quarter calls to him. "Ho there!
Come, come, thou Oedipus, why stay we yet?
Long time thy footsteps linger on the way."
And he, when he perceived the God had called,
Bade Theseus come, the ruler of the land;
And when he came, he said, "Ah, dearest friend,
Give me thy hand's old pledge to these my girls;
And ye, give yours to him. And do thou swear,
Of thy free will never to give them up,
But ever to fulfil what thou shalt judge,
With clearest insight, best." And he, as one
Of noble nature, wept not, but did vow
With solemn oath to do his friend's behest.
And this being done, then straightway Oedipus
Clasping his children with his sightless hands,
Spake thus: "My children! Now ye need to show
Your tempers true and noble, and withdraw
From where ye stand, nor think it right to look
On things that best are hidden, nor to list
To those that speak; but ye, with utmost speed
Go forth. But Theseus, who may claim the right,

Let him remain, to learn the things that come."
So much we all together heard him speak,
And then, with tears fast flowing, groaning still
We followed with the maidens. Going on
A little space we turned. And lo! we saw
The man no more; but he, the King, was there,
Holding his hand to shade his eyes, as one
To whom there comes a vision drear and dread
He may not bear to look on. Yet awhile,
But little, and we see him bowed to earth,
Adoring it, and in the self-same prayer
Olympus, home of Gods. What form of death
He died, knows no man, but our Theseus only.
For neither was it thunderbolt from Zeus
With flashing fire that slew him, nor the blast
Of whirlwind sweeping o'er the sea that hour,
But either some one whom the Gods had sent,
To guide his steps, or else the abyss of earth
In friendly mood had opened wide its jaws
Without one pang. And so the man was led
With nought to mourn for—did not leave the world
As worn with pain and sickness; but his end,
If any ever was, was wonderful.
And if I seem to any, saying this,
As one who dreams, I would not care to win
Their favour who as dreamer count of me.

CHORUS: Where are his daughters, and the friends that led them?

MESSENGER: Not far are they. Their voices wailing loud
Give token clear that they are drawing nigh.

(Enter Antigone and Ismene.)

133

Strophe

ANTIGONE: Ah me! 'tis ours to mourn,
        All desolate and sad,
        Not once or twice alone,
        Our father's taint of blood,
    For whom long time we bore our constant toil
    In many a land, and now at last must tell,
        Seeing and suffering both,
        Woes strange and wonderful.

CHORUS: What is it then?

ANTIGONE: That, friends, ye well may guess.

CHORUS: Has he then gone?

ANTIGONE: As thou might'st wish to go:
        How else? since he was one
        Whom neither din of war,
        Nor fell disease approached;
        Whom, with strange darking fate
        The land of shadows clasped,
        So borne away from us:
        And lo! upon our eyes
        There falls the night of death!
        For how, on some far land
        Wandering, or ocean wave,
    Shall we now live our life intolerable?

ISMENE: I know not that indeed!
    But oh! that Hades dark and murderous
        Would take me in my woe,
    To die with him, my father, in his age!
    Henceforth my life is more than I can live.

CHORUS: O children! noblest pair!

Ye ought to bear right well
That which bears God's intent.
Be not thus vexed in mood;
The path ye trod is one ye should not blame.

Antistrophe

ANTIGONE: Even o'er grief long borne
We lingered with regret,
And that which erst we loved not,
Became the thing we loved;
So was it when I had him in my grasp.
My father, dearest one!
O thou, who now art wrapt
In that eternal darkness of the grave!
For never shall thy name, though thou art dead,
To her and me be anything but dear!

CHORUS: And did he fare . . . ?

ANTIGONE: He fared as he desired.

CHORUS: And how was that?

ANTIGONE: In strange land as he wished
He died, and sleeps beneath,
Where sweet, calm shadows brood for evermore;
Nor did he die unwept;
For still these eyes, my father, shed their tears,
Nor know I, in my woe,
How to suppress my grief, my grief for thee.
Ah me! thou did'st desire
In this strange land to die;
And yet thou thus hast died,
Alone, apart from me!

ISMENE: Ah me! ah misery!

What fate of loneliness,
What drear perplexity,
Awaits me now, and thee, O dearest one,
In this our orphaned lot?

CHORUS: Yet, maidens, since his life
With blessing now has closed;
Cease from your wailing drear;
No man escapes from woe.

ANTIGONE: Once more, dear sister, let us haste away.

ISMENE: With what intent?

ANTIGONE: A strong desire comes o'er me.

ISMENE: What is't?

ANTIGONE: To see once more the holy ground.

ISMENE: Of whom?

ANTIGONE: My father. Woe is me! Ah, woe!

ISMENE: But how can this be right? And seest thou not . . . . ?

ANTIGONE: What means this chiding?

ISMENE: This too . . . . ?

ANTIGONE: This again?

ISMENE: He died unburied, none were by his side.

ANTIGONE: Lead me, and slay me o'er him.

ISMENE: Woe is me!
Where then shall I, abandoned and perplexed,
Drag on my weary life?

CHORUS: Fear nothing, maidens dear!

ANTIGONE: Where escape?

CHORUS: Yet one escape there was . . . .

ANTIGONE: Of what speak'st thou?

CHORUS: Of thine and hers, from chance of evil fate.

ANTIGONE: I think this o'er. . . . .

CHORUS: O'er what then broodest thou?

ANTIGONE: How to return to what was once our home
           I find not.

CHORUS: Seek it not.

ANTIGONE: Yet woes oppress.

CHORUS: Long since they crushed thee.

ANTIGONE: Desperate then; now worse.

CHORUS: A sea of troubles, then, has been your lot.

ANTIGONE: Yea, yea.

CHORUS: I own it too!

ANTIGONE: Ah me! ah me!
               Whither to turn, O Zeus?
               For still, e'en now, the God
               Leads me to bodings strange.

           (*Enter Theseus.*)

THESEUS: Cease from your weeping, maidens. Over those
           For whom the night of death as blessing comes,
           We may not mourn. Such grief the Gods chastise.

ANTIGONE: O son of Aegeus, at thy feet we fall.

THESEUS: What boon then seek ye, maidens?

ANTIGONE: We would see

With our own eyes our father's sepulchre.

THESEUS: It may not be: ye may not thither go.

ANTIGONE: How say'st thou, prince, of Athens lord and king?

THESEUS: O maidens, he forbade that mortal foot
Should e'er draw nigh this spot, or mortal voice
Invoke in prayer the holy burial-place
Where now he lies. And, doing this, he said
That I should rule a land unvexed by ills;
These things our God has heard, and that dread Power,
The Oath of Zeus, that ever heareth all.

ANTIGONE: This shall suffice, if this was what he willed.
But send thou us to Thebes of old renown,
That so, if it may be, we stop the death
That comes upon our brothers.

THESEUS: This will I
Accomplish for you, and whate'er is best
For you, and dear to him who sleeps below,
So lately gone, I may not weary in.

CHORUS: Refrain ye then from weeping, cease to mourn.
All this is fixed, and nought of all shall fail.

SOPHOCLES

❖❖❖❖❖❖❖❖❖

Antigone

Translated by Robert Whitelaw

CHARACTERS IN THE PLAY

ANTIGONE ⎫
ISMENE ⎭ *daughters of Oedipus*

CREON, *king of Thebes*

A SENTINEL

HAEMON, *son of Creon*

TEIRESIAS, *a blind prophet*

A MESSENGER

EURYDICE, *the wife of Creon*

SECOND MESSENGER

CHORUS *of Theban Elders*

ARGUMENT

Eteocles, the son of Oedipus and king of Thebes, had exiled his brother Polyneices. Polyneices raised an army at Argos and led it against his native city. In the battle that followed, the two brothers fell each by the other's hand. Thus was fulfilled the curse which Oedipus, at Colonus, had pronounced upon his sons. The play opens on the day after the battle. Creon, who has become king, raises unwittingly the question of the relation between man's law and God's by decreeing that the body of Eteocles, who had died defending his city, may be buried, while that of Polyneices shall be left a prey to birds and dogs. Logicality, we learn, is wrong; instinct and tradition are right.

An open space before the palace at Thebes. Antigone and Ismene enter.

ANTIGONE: O Sister-Life, Ismene's, twin with mine,
Knowest thou of the burden of our race
Aught that from us yet living Zeus holds back?
Nay, for nought grievous and nought ruinous,
No shame and no dishonour, have I not seen
Poured on our hapless heads, both thine and mine.
And even now what edict hath the prince
Uttered, men say, to all this Theban folk?
Thou knowest it and hast heard? or 'scapes thy sense,
Aimed at thy friends, the mischief of thy foes?

ISMENE: To me of friends, Antigone, no word
Hath come, or sweet or bitter, since that we
Two sisters of two brothers were bereaved,
Both on a day slain by a twofold blow:
And, now that vanished is the Argive host
Ev'n with the night fled hence, I know no more,
If that I fare the better or the worse.

ANTIGONE: I knew full well, and therefore from the gates
O' the court I led thee hither, alone to hear.

ISMENE: There's trouble in thy looks: thy tidings tell.

ANTIGONE: Yea, hath not Creon, of our two brothers slain,
Honoured with burial one, disdained the other?
For Eteocles, they say, he in the earth
With all fair rites and ceremony hath laid,
Nor lacks he honour in the world below;
But the poor dust of Polyneices dead

Through Thebes, 'tis said, the edict has gone forth
That none may bury, none make moan for him,
But leave unwept, untombed, a dainty prize
For ravening birds that gloat upon their prey.
So hath our good lord Creon to thee and me
Published, men say, his pleasure—ay, to *me*—
And hither comes, to all who know it not
Its purport to make plain, nor deems the thing
Of slight account, but, whoso does this deed,
A public death by stoning is his doom.
Thou hast it now; and quickly shall be proved
If thou art noble, or base from noble strain.

ISMENE: O rash of heart, if this indeed be so,
What help in me, to loosen or to bind?

ANTIGONE: Consider, toil and pain if thou wilt share.

ISMENE: On what adventure bound? What wouldst thou do?

ANTIGONE: To lift his body, wilt thou join with me?

ISMENE: Wouldst thou indeed rebel, and bury him?

ANTIGONE: My brother I will bury, and thine no less,
Whether thou wilt or no: no traitress I.

ISMENE: O all too bold—when Creon hath forbid?

ANTIGONE: My rights to hinder is no right of his.

ISMENE: Ah, sister, yet think how our father died,
Wrapt in what cloud of hate and ignominy
By his own sins, self-proved, and both his eyes
With suicidal hand himself he stabbed:
Then too his mother-wife, two names in one,
Fordid with twisted noose her woful life:
Last, our two brothers in one fatal day
Drew sword, O miserable, and each to each

142

Dealt mutual slaughter with unnatural hands:
And now shall we twain, who alone are left,
Fall like the rest, and worse—in spite of law,
And scorning kings, their edicts and their power?
Oh rather let us think, 'tis not for us,
Who are but women, to contend with men:
And the King's word is mighty, and to this,
And harsher words than this, we needs must bow.
Therefore will I, imploring of the dead
Forgiveness, that I yield but as I must,
Obey the King's commandment: for with things
Beyond our reach 'twere foolishness to meddle.

ANTIGONE: I'll neither urge thee, nor, if now thou'dst help
My doing, should I thank thee for thine aid.
Do thou after thy kind: thy choice is made:
I'll bury him; doing this, so let me die.
So with my loved one loved shall I abide,
My crime a deed most holy: for the dead
Longer have I to please than these on earth.
There I shall dwell for ever: be it thine
To have scorned what gods have hallowed, if thou wilt.

ISMENE: Nay, nothing do I scorn: but, how to break
My country's law—I am witless of the way.

ANTIGONE: Be this thy better part: I go to heap
The earth upon my brother, whom I love.

ISMENE: Alas, unhappy, how I fear for thee!

ANTIGONE: Fear not for me: guide thine own fate aright.

ISMENE: Yet breathe this purpose to no ear but mine:
Keep thou thy counsel well—and so will I.

ANTIGONE: Oh speak: for much more hatred thou wilt get,
Concealing, than proclaiming it to all.

143

ISMENE: This fever at thy heart by frost is fed.

ANTIGONE: But, whom I most should please, they most are pleased.

ISMENE: So wouldst thou: but thou canst not as thou wouldst.

ANTIGONE: Why, then, when strength shall fail me, I will cease.

ISMENE: Not to attempt the impossible is best.

ANTIGONE: Hated by me, and hated by the dead—
               To him a hateful presence evermore—
               Thou shouldst be, and thou shalt be, speaking thus.
               But leave me, and the folly that is mine,
               This worst to suffer—not the worst—since still
               A worse remains, no noble death to die.

ISMENE: Go if thou wilt: but going know thyself
               Senseless, yet to thy friends a friend indeed.

               (*Exeunt. Enter Chorus of Theban Elders.*)

               Strophe 1

CHORUS: Lo, the sun upspringing!
               Fairest light we hail thee
               Of all dawns that on Thebes the seven-gated
               Ever broke! Eye of golden day!
               Over Dirce's fount appearing,
               Hence the Argive host white-shielded,
               That in complete arms came hither,
               Headlong homeward thou didst urge
               Faster still with shaken rein.
               At call of Polyneices, stirred
               By bitter heat of wrangling claims,
               Against our land they gathered, and they swooped
               Down on us—like an eagle, screaming hoarse,

White-clad, with wings of snow—
With shields a many and with waving crests.

Antistrophe 1

But above our dwellings,
With his spears that thirsted
For our blood, at each gate's mouth of the seven
Gaping round, paused the foe—and went,
Ere his jaws with blood were sated,
Or our circling towers the torch-flame
Caught and kindled: so behind him
Raged intense the battle-din—
While for life the Serpent fought.
For Zeus the tongue of vaunting pride
Hates with exceeding hate; he marked
That torrent army's onward flood, superb
With clank of gold, and with his brandished fire
Smote down who foremost climbed
To shout his triumph on our ramparts' heights.

Strophe 2

Hurled from that height with swift reverse,
The unpitying earth received him as he fell,
And quenched the brand he fain had flung,
And quelled the mad endeavour,
The frantic storm-gusts of his windy hate.
So fared it then with him;
Nor less elsewhere great Ares dealt
Against the foemen thunderous blows—
Our trace-horse on the right.
For seven chieftains at our seven gates
Met each his equal foe: and Zeus,

Who foiled their onset, claims from all his due,
The brazen arms, which on the field they left:
Save that infuriate pair,
Who, from one father and one mother sprung,
Against each other laid in rest
Their spears, victorious both,
And each by other share one equal death.

Antistrophe 2

But now of Victory be glad:
She meets our gladness with an answering smile,
And Thebes, the many-charioted,
Hears far resound her praises:
Now then with war have done, and strife forget!
All temples of the gods
Fill we with song and night-long dance;
And, Theban Bacchus, this our mirth
Lead thou, and shake the earth!
But lo the ruler of this Theban land,
Son of Menoeceus, Creon comes,
Crowned by these new and strange events, he comes—
By will of heav'n our new-created King,
What counsel pondering?
Who by his sovereign will hath now convoked,
In solemn conference to meet,
The elders of the state;
Obedient to whose summons, we are here.

(*Enter Creon.*)

CREON: Sirs, it hath pleased the gods to right again
Our Theban fortunes, by sore tempest tossed:
And by my messenger I summoned hither

You out of all the state; first, as I knew you
To the might o' the throne of Laius loyal ever:
Also, when Oedipus upheld the state,
And when he perished, to their children still
Ye with a constant mind were faithful found:
Now they are gone: both on one fatal field
An equal guilt atoned with equal doom,
Slayers of each other, by each other slain:
And I am left, the nearest to their blood,
To wield alone the sceptre and the realm.
There is no way to know of any man
The spirit and the wisdom and the will,
Till he stands proved, ruler and lawgiver.
For who, with a whole city to direct,
Yet cleaves not to those counsels that are best,
But locks his lips in silence, being afraid,
I held and hold him ever of men most base:
And whoso greater than his country's cause
Esteems a friend, I count him nothing worth.
For, Zeus who seeth all be witness now,
Nor for the safety's sake would I keep silence,
And see the ruin on my country fall,
Nor would I deem an enemy to the state
Friend to myself; remembering still that she,
She only brings us safe; her deck we pace,
Unfoundered 'mid the storm, our friends and we.
So for the good of Thebes her laws I'll frame:
And such the proclamation I set forth,
Touching the sons of Oedipus, ev'n now—
Eteocles, who fighting for this land
In battle has fall'n, more valiant none than he,
To bury, and no funeral rite omit,
To brave men paid—their solace in the grave:
Not so his brother, Polyneices: he,

From exile back returning, utterly
With fire his country and his fathers' gods
Would fain have burnt, fain would with kinsmen's blood
Have slaked his thirst, or dragged us captive hence:
Therefore to all this city it is proclaimed
That none may bury, none make moan for him,
But leave him lying all ghastly where he fell,
Till fowls o' the air and dogs have picked his bones.
So am I purposed: not at least by me
Shall traitors be preferred to honest men:
But, whoso loves this city, him indeed
I shall not cease to honour, alive or dead.

CHORUS: Creon, son of Menoeceus, 'tis thy pleasure
The friend and foe of Thebes so to requite:
And, whatso pleases thee, that same is law,
Both for our Theban dead and us who live.

CREON: Look to it, then, my bidding is performed.

CHORUS: Upon some younger man impose this burden.

CREON: To watch the body, sentinels are set.

CHORUS: What service more then wouldst thou lay on us?

CREON: That ye resist whoever disobeys.

CHORUS: Who is so senseless that desires to die?

CREON: The penalty is death: yet hopes deceive,
And men wax foolish oft through greed of gain.

(*Enter a Sentinel.*)

SENTINEL: That I come hither, King, nimble of foot,
And breathless with my haste, I'll not profess:
For many a doubtful halt upon the way,

And many a wheel to the right-about, I had,
Oft as my prating heart gave counsel, "Fool,
What ails thee going into the lion's mouth?"
Then, "Blockhead, wilt thou tarry? If Creon learns
This from another man, shalt thou not smart?"
So doubtfully I fared—much haste, scant speed—
And, if the way was short, 'twas long to me.
But to come hither to thee prevailed at last,
And, though the speech be nought, yet I will speak.
For I have come fast clutching at the hope
That nought's to suffer but what fate decrees.

CREON: What is it that hath troubled thus thy mind?

SENTINEL: First for myself this let me say: the deed
I neither did, nor saw who was the doer,
And 'twere not just that I should suffer harm.

CREON: Wisely, thyself in covert, at the mark
Thou aimest: some shrewd news, methinks, thou'lt tell.

SENTINEL: Danger to face, well may a man be cautious.

CREON: Speak then, and go thy way, and make an end.

SENTINEL: Now I will speak. Some one ev'n now hath buried
The body and is gone; with thirsty dust
Sprinkling it o'er, and paying observance due.

CREON: How? By what man was dared a deed so rash?

SENTINEL: I cannot tell. No mattock's stroke indeed,
Nor spade's upcast was there: hard was the ground,
Baked dry, unbroken: track of chariot-wheels
Was none, nor any sign who did this thing.
But he who kept the watch at earliest dawn
Showed to us all—a mystery, hard to clear.
Not buried was the dead man, but concealed,

With dust besprinkled, as for fear of sin:
And neither of dog, nor any beast of prey,
That came, that tore the body, found we trace.
Then bitter words we bandied to and fro,
Denouncing each the other; and soon to blows
Our strife had grown—was none would keep the peace—
For every one was guilty of the deed,
And none confessed, but all denied they knew.
And we were fain to handle red-hot iron,
Or walk through fire barefoot, or swear by heaven,
That neither had we done it, nor had shared
His secret with who planned it or who wrought.
So all in vain we questioned: and at last
One spake, and all who heard him, bowed by fear,
Bent to the earth their faces, knowing not
How to gainsay, nor doing what he said
How we might 'scape mischance. This deed to thee
He urged that we should show, and hide it not.
And his advice prevailed; and by the lot
To luckless me this privilege befell.
Unwilling and unwelcome is my errand,
A bearer of ill news, whom no man loves.

CHORUS: O King, my thought hath counselled me long since,
Haply this deed is ordered by the gods.

CREON: Cease, ere my wrath is kindled at thy speech,
Lest thou be found an old man and a fool.
Intolerably thou pratest of the gods,
That they to yonder dead man have respect.
Yea, for what service with exceeding honour
Sought they his burial, who came here to burn
Their pillared shrines and temple-offerings,
And of their land and of their laws make havoc?
Or seest thou that the gods allow the wicked?

Not so: but some impatient of my will
Among my people made a murmuring,
Shaking their heads in secret, to the yoke
With stubborn necks unbent, and hearts disloyal.
Full certainly I know that they with bribes
Have on these men prevailed to do this deed.
Of all the evils current in this world
Most mischievous is gold. This hath laid waste
Fair cities, and unpeopled homes of men:
Many an honest heart hath the false lure
Of gold seduced to walk in ways of shame;
And hence mankind are versed in villanies,
And of all godless acts have learnt the lore.
But, who took hire to execute this work,
Wrought to their own undoing at the last.
Since, if the dread of Zeus I still revere,
Be well assured—and what I speak I swear—
Unless the author of this burial
Ye find, and in my sight produce him here,
For you mere death shall not suffice, until
Gibbeted alive this outrage ye disclose,
That ye may know what gains are worth the winning,
And henceforth clutch the wiselier, having learnt
That to seek gain in all things is not well.
For from ill-gotten pelf the lives of men
Ruined than saved more often shall ye see.

SENTINEL: May I speak a word, or thus am I dismissed?

CREON: Know'st thou not that ev'n now thy voice offends?

SENTINEL: Do I afflict thy hearing or thy heart?

CREON: Where I am pained, it skills not to define.

SENTINEL: The doer grieves thy mind, but I thine ears.

CREON: That thou wast born to chatter, 'tis too plain.

SENTINEL: And therefore not the doer of this deed.

CREON: At thy life's cost thou didst it, bought with gold.

SENTINEL: Alas!
          'Tis pity, men should judge, yet judge amiss.

CREON: Talk you of "judging" glibly as you may—
          Who did this deed, I'll know, or ye shall own
          That all your wondrous winnings end in loss.

SENTINEL: With all my heart I wish he may be found:
          But found or no—for that's as fortune will—
          I shall not show my face to you again.
          Great cause I have to thank the gracious gods,
          Saved past all hope and reckoning even now.

          (*Exeunt Creon and the Sentinel.*)

          Strophe 1

CHORUS: Many are the wonders of the world,
          And none so wonderful as Man.
          Over the waters wan
          His storm-vext bark he steers,
          While the fierce billows break
          Round his path, and o'er his head:
          And the Earth-mother, first of gods,
          The ageless, the indomitable,
          With his ploughing to and fro
          He wearieth, year by year:
          In the deep furrow toil the patient mules.

Antistrophe 1

The birds o' the air he snares and takes,
All the light-hearted fluttering race:
And tribes of savage beasts,
And creatures of the deep,
Meshed in his woven toils,
Own the master-mind of man.
Free lives of upland and of wild
By human arts are curbed and tamed:
See the horse's shaggy neck
Submissive to the yoke—
And strength untired of mountain-roaming bulls.

Strophe 2

Language withal he learnt,
And Thought that as the wind is free,
And aptitudes of civic life:
Ill-lodged no more he lies,
His roof the sky, the earth his bed,
Screened now from piercing frost and pelting rain;
All-fertile in resource, resourceless never
Meets he the morrow; only death
He wants the skill to shun:
But many a fell disease the healer's art hath foiled.

Antistrophe 2

So soaring far past hope,
The wise inventiveness of man
Finds diverse issues, good and ill:
If from their course he wrests
The firm foundations of the state,

Laws, and the justice he is sworn to keep,
High in the city, citiless I deem him,
Dealing with baseness: overbold,
May he my hearth avoid,
Nor let my thoughts with his, who does such deeds, agree!

(*Enter the Sentinel with Antigone.*)

What strange portentous sight is this,
I doubt my eyes, beholding? This—
How shall I gainsay what I know?—
This maiden *is*—Antigone!
Daughter of Oedipus,
Hapless child of a hapless sire,
What hast thou done? It cannot be
That thou hast transgressed the King's command—
That, taken in folly, *thee* they bring!

SENTINEL: This same is she that did the burial:
We caught her in the act. But where's the King?

CHORUS: Back from the palace in good time he comes.

(*Enter Creon.*)

CREON: What chance is this, to which my steps are timed?

SENTINEL: Nothing, sir King, should men swear not to do;
For second thoughts to first thoughts give the lie.
Hither, I made full sure, I scarce should come
Back, by your threats beruffled as I was.
Yet here, surprised by most unlooked-for joy,
That trifles all delights that e'er I knew,
I bring you—though my coming breaks my oath—
This maiden, whom, busied about the corpse,
We captured. This time were no lots to throw:

154

My own good fortune this, and none but mine.
Now therefore, King, take her yourself and try her,
And question as you will: but I have earned
Full clearance and acquittal of this coil.

CREON: Where, on what manner, was your captive taken?

SENTINEL: Burying the man, we took her: all is told.

CREON: Art thou advised of this? Is it the truth?

SENTINEL: I say I saw her burying the body,
That you forbade. Is that distinct and clear?

CREON: How was she seen, and taken in the act?

SENTINEL: So it fell out. When I had gone from hence,
With thy loud threats yet sounding in my ears,
We swept off all the dust that hid the limbs,
And to the light stripped bare the clammy corpse,
And on the hill's brow sat, and faced the wind,
Choosing a spot clear of the body's stench.
Roundly we chid each other to the work;
"No sleeping at your post there" was our word.
So did we keep the watch, till in mid-heaven
The sun's bright-burning orb above us hung,
With fierce noon-heat: and now a sudden blast
Swept, and a storm of dust, that vexed the sky
And choked the plain, and all the leaves o' the trees
O' the plain were marred, and the wide heaven it filled:
We with shut eyes the heaven-sent plague endured.
And, when after long time its force was spent,
We saw this maiden, and a bitter cry
She poured, as of a wailing bird that sees
Her empty nest dismantled of its brood:
So she, when she espied the body bare,
Cried out and wept, and many a grievous curse

155

Upon their heads invoked by whom 'twas done.
And thirsty dust she sprinkled with her hands,
And lifted up an urn, fair-wrought of brass,
And with thrice-poured libations crowned the dead.
We saw it and we hasted, and at once,
All undismayed, our captive, hemmed her round,
And with the two offences charged her there,
Both first and last. Nothing did she deny,
But made me glad and sorry, owning all.
For to have slipped one's own neck from the noose
Is sweet, yet no one likes to get his friends
In trouble: but my nature is to make
All else of small account, so I am safe.

CREON: Speak thou, who bendest on the earth thy gaze,
Are these things, which are witnessed, true or false?

ANTIGONE: Not false, but true: that which he saw, he speaks.

CREON: So, sirrah, thou are free; go where thou wilt,
Loosed from the burden of this heavy charge.

(*Exit the Sentinel.*)

But tell me thou—and let thy speech be brief—
The edict hadst thou heard, which this forbade?

ANTIGONE: I could not choose but hear what all men heard.

CREON: And didst thou dare to disobey the law?

ANTIGONE: Nowise from Zeus, methought, this edict came,
Nor Justice, that abides among the gods
In Hades, who ordained these laws for men.
Nor did I deem *thine* edicts of such force
That they, a mortal's bidding, should o'erride
Unwritten laws, eternal in the heavens.
Not of to-day or yesterday are these,

156

But live from everlasting, and from whence
They sprang, none knoweth. I would not, for the breach
Of these, through fear of any human pride,
To heaven atone. I knew that I must die:
How else? Without thine edict, that were so.
And if before my time, why, this were gain.
Compassed about with ills, who lives, as I,
Death, to such life as his, must needs be gain.
So is it to me to undergo this doom
No grief at all: but had I left my brother,
My mother's child, unburied where he lay,
Then I had grieved; but now this grieves me not.
Senseless I seem to thee, so doing? Belike
A senseless judgment finds me void of sense.

CHORUS: How in the child the sternness of the sire
            Shows stern, before the storm untaught to bend!

CREON: Yet know full well that such o'er-stubborn wills
            Are broken most of all, as sturdiest steel,
            Of an untempered hardness, fresh from forge,
            Most surely snapped and shivered should ye see.
            Lo how a little curb has strength enough
            To tame the restive horse: for to a slave
            His masters give no license to be proud.
            Insult on insult heaped! Was't not enough
            My promulgated laws to have transgressed,
            But, having done it, face to face with me
            She boasts of this and glories in the deed?
            I surely am the woman, she the man,
            If she defies my power, and I submit.
            Be she my sister's child, or sprung from one
            More near of blood than all my house to me,
            Not so shall they escape my direst doom—
            She and her sister: for I count her too

Guilty no less of having planned this work.
Go, call her hither: in the house I saw her
Raving ev'n now, nor mistress of her thoughts.
So oft the mind, revolving secret crime,
Makes premature disclosure of its guilt.
But this is hateful, when the guilty one,
Detected, thinks to glorify his fault.

ANTIGONE: To kill me—wouldst thou more with me than this?

CREON: This is enough: I do desire no more.

ANTIGONE: Why dost thou then delay? I have no pleasure
To hear thee speak—have not and would not have:
Nor less distasteful is my speech to thee.
Yet how could I have won myself a praise
More honourable than this, of burying
My brother? This from every voice should win
Approval, might but fear men's lips unseal.
But kings are fortunate—not least in this,
That they may do and speak what things they will.

CREON: All Thebes sees this with other eyes than thine.

ANTIGONE: They see as I, but bate their breath to thee.

CREON: And art thou not ashamed, from them to differ?

ANTIGONE: To reverence a brother is not shameful.

CREON: And was not he who died for Thebes thy brother?

ANTIGONE: One mother bore us, and one sire begat.

CREON: Yet, honouring both, thou dost dishonour him.

ANTIGONE: He in the grave will not subscribe to this.

CREON: How, if no less thou dost revere the guilty?

ANTIGONE: 'Twas not his slave that perished, but his brother.

CREON: The enemy of this land: its champion, he.

ANTIGONE: Yet Death of due observance must not fail.

CREON: Just and unjust urge not an equal claim.

ANTIGONE: Perchance in Hades 'tis a holy deed.

CREON: Hatred, not ev'n in death, converts to love.

ANTIGONE: Not in your hates, but in your loves, I'd share.

CREON: Go to the shades, and, if thou'lt love, love there:
No woman, while I live, shall master me.

(Enter Ismene.)

CHORUS: See, from the palace comes Ismene—
Sisterly drops from her eyes down-shedding:
Clouded her brows droop, heavy with sorrow;
And the blood-red tinge of a burning blush
Covers her beautiful downcast face.

CREON: Thou, who hast crept, a serpent in my home,
Draining my blood, unseen; and I knew not
Rearing two pests, to overset my throne;
Speak—wilt thou too confess that in this work
Thou hadst a hand, or swear thou didst not know?

ISMENE: I'll say the deed was mine, if she consents:
My share of the blame I bear, and do not shrink.

ANTIGONE: Justice forbids thy claim; neither didst thou
Agree, nor I admit thee to my counsels.

ISMENE: I am not ashamed, in thine extremity,
To make myself companion of thy fate.

ANTIGONE: Whose was the deed, know Hades and the dead:
I love not friends, who talk of friendliness.

ISMENE: Sister, disdain me not, but let me pour
My blood with thine, an offering to the dead.

ANTIGONE: Leave me to die alone, nor claim the work
Thou wouldst not help. My death will be enough.

ISMENE: What joy have I to live, when thou art gone?

ANTIGONE: Ask Creon that: thou art of kin to him.

ISMENE: Why wilt thou grieve me with thy needless taunts?

ANTIGONE: If I mock thee, 'tis with a heavy heart.

ISMENE: What may I do to serve thee even now?

ANTIGONE: Look to thyself: I grudge thee not thy safety.

ISMENE: And may I not, unhappy, share thy death?

ANTIGONE: Thou didst make choice to live, but I to die.

ISMENE: Might I unsay my words, this were not so.

ANTIGONE: Wise seemed we—thou to these, and I to those.

ISMENE: But now our fault is equal, thine and mine.

ANTIGONE: Take heart to live: for so thou dost: but I—
Dead is my life long since—to help the dead.

CREON: One of these two, methinks, proves foolish now;
The other's folly with her life began.

ISMENE: Nay, for, O King, misfortunes of the wise
To madness turn the wisdom that they have.

CREON: 'Tis so with thee, choosing to share her guilt.

ISMENE: How should I live alone, without my sister?

CREON: Call her not thine: thou hast no sister now.

ISMENE: But wilt thou tear her from thy son's embrace?

CREON: Are there no women in the world but she?

ISMENE: Not as their faith was plighted, each to each.

CREON: An evil wife I like not for my son.

ANTIGONE: Haemon! beloved! hear not thy father's scorn.

CREON: Thou and thy love to me are wearisome.

CHORUS: Wilt thou indeed snatch from thy son his bride?

CREON: 'Tis death that will unloose their marriage-bond.

CHORUS: It seems thou art resolved that she must die?

CREON: Of that we are agreed. Delay no more:
Ye, servants, lead them in. For from this time
Women they needs must be, and range no more:
Since ev'n the bold may play the runaway,
When death he sees close-creeping on his life.

(Exeunt Antigone and Ismene.)

Strophe 1

CHORUS: Happy indeed is the life of the man who tastes not of
trouble!
For when from the gods a house is shaken,
Fails nevermore the curse,
On most and on least of the race descending:
Like to a rolling wave,
By furious blasts from the Thraceward driven—
Out of the nethermost deeps, out of the fathomless gloom,
Casting up mire and blackness and storm-vext wrack of
the sea—
And back, with a moan like thunder, from the cliffs the
surf is hurled.

Antistrophe 1

So from of old to the Labdacid race comes sorrow on
  sorrow:
And, ev'n as the dead, so fare the living:
Respite from ills is none,
Nor one generation redeems another—
All will some god bring low.
Now o'er the last root of the house, fate-stricken,
Woe for the light that had shined, woe for the lingering
  hope!
Smooth over all is lying the blood-stained dust they have
  spread—
Rash speech, and a frantic purpose, and the gods who
  reign below.

Strophe 2

What human trespass, Zeus,
May circumscribe thy power,
Which neither sleep o'ercomes,
That saps the strength of all things else,
Nor months that run their tireless course,
But thou for ever with an ageless sway
The dazzling splendour dost possess
Of thine Olympian home?
'Tis now as it hath ever been,
And still in years to come
The old order will not change:
Never from human life departs
The universal scourge of man,
His own presumptuous pride.

Antistrophe 2

Hope wings her daring flight,
By strong winds borne afar—
And some are blessed; and some
Are cheated of their vain desires,
That learn their folly all too late,
When in the fire they tread with scorchèd feet.
'Twas said of old—and time approves
The wisdom of the saw—
That, when in foolish ways, that end
In ruin, gods would lead
A mortal's mind astray,
Evil that man miscalls his good:
A brief while then he holds his course
By fatuous pride unscathed.
See, thy son Haemon comes hither, of all
Thy children the last. Comes he lamenting
The doom of the maiden, his bride Antigone—
And the frustrated hope of his marriage?

(*Enter Haemon.*)

CREON: Soon we shall know, better than seers could say.
My son, in anger art thou come to me,
Hearing the sentence, not to be reversed,
Which on thy destined bride I have pronounced?
Or am I still thy friend, do what I may?

HAEMON: Father, I am in thy hand: with thy wise counsels
Thou dost direct me; these I shall obey.
Not rightly should I deem of more account
The winning of a wife than thy good guidance.

CREON: Be this thy dearest wish and next thy heart,

In all things to uphold thy father's will.
For to this end men crave to see grow up
Obedient children round them in their homes,
Both to requite their enemies with hate,
And render equal honour to their friends.
Whoso begets unprofitable children,
What shall be said of him, but that he gets
Grief for himself, loud laughter for his foes?
Never, my son, let for a woman's sake
Reason give way to sense, but know full well
Cold is the pleasure that he clasps, who woos
An evil woman to his board and bed.
What wounds so deeply as an evil friend?
Count then this maiden as thine enemy,
Loathe her, and give her leave, in that dark world
To which she goes, to marry with another.
For out of all the city since I found
Her only, and her openly, rebellious,
I shall not to the city break my word,
But she shall die. Let her appeal to Zeus,
And sing the sanctity of kindred blood—
What then? If in my own house I shall nurse
Rebellion, how shall strangers not rebel?
He who to his own kith and kin does right,
Will in the state deal righteously with all.
Of such a man I shall not fear to boast,
Well he can rule, and well he would obey,
And in the storm of battle at his post
Firm he would stand, a comrade staunch and true.
But praise from me that man shall never have,
Who either boldly thrusts aside the law
Or takes upon him to instruct his rulers,
Whom, by the state empowered, he should obey,
In little and in much, in right and wrong.

The worst of evils is to disobey.
Cities by this are ruined, homes of men
Made desolate by this; this in the battle
Breaks into headlong rout the wavering line;
The steadfast ranks, the many lives unhurt,
Are to obedience due. We must defend
The government and order of the state,
And not be governed by a wilful girl.
We'll yield our place up, if we must, to men;
To women that we stooped, shall not be said.

CHORUS: Unless an old man's judgment is at fault,
These words of thine, we deem, are words of wisdom.

HAEMON: Reason, my father, in the mind of man,
Noblest of all their gifts, the gods implant,
And how to find thy reasoning at fault,
I know not, and to learn I should be loth;
Yet for another it might not be amiss.
But I for thee am vigilant to mark
All that men say, or do, or find to blame.
Thy presence awes the simple citizen
From speaking words that shall not please thine ear,
But I hear what they whisper in the dark,
And how the city for this maid laments,
That of all women she the least deserving
Dies for most glorious deeds a death most cruel,
Who her own brother, fall'n among the slain,
Left not unburied there, to be devoured
By ravening dogs or any bird o' the air:—
"Should not her deed be blazoned all in gold?"
Upon the darkness still such whisper grows.
But I of all possessions that I have
Prize most, my father, thy prosperity.
Welldoing and fair fame of sire to son,

Of son to sire, is noblest ornament.
Cleave not, I pray thee, to this constant mind,
That what thou sayest, and nought beside, is truth.
For men who think that only they are wise,
None eloquent, right-minded none, but they,
Often, when searched, prove empty. 'Tis no shame,
Ev'n if a man be wise, that he should yet
Learn many things, and not hold out too stiffly.
Beside the torrent's course, of trees that bend
Each bough, thou seest, and every twig is safe;
Those that resist are by the roots uptorn.
And ships, that brace with stubborn hardihood
Their mainsheet to the gale, pursue their voyage
Keel-uppermost, their sailors' thwarts reversed.
Cease from thy wrath; be not inexorable:
For if despite my youth I too may think
My thought, I'll say that best it is by far
That men should be all-knowing if they may,
But if—as oft the scale inclines not so—
Why then, by good advice 'tis good to learn.

CHORUS: What in thy son's speech, King, is seasonable
'Tis fit thou shouldst receive: and thou in his:
For there is reason in the words of both.

CREON: Shall I, grown grey with age, be taught indeed—
And by this boy—to think what he thinks right?

HAEMON: Nothing that is not right: though I am young,
Consider not my years, but how I act.

CREON: Is this thine act—to honour the unruly?

HAEMON: Wrongdoers, dishonour—outrage, if thou wilt!

CREON: Hath not this maiden caught this malady?

HAEMON: The general voice of Thebes says no to that.

166

CREON:	Shall Thebes prescribe to me how I must govern?
HAEMON:	How all too young art thou in speaking thus!
CREON:	Whose business is't but mine how Thebes is governed?
HAEMON:	A city is none, that to one man belongs.
CREON:	Is it not held, the city is the king's?
HAEMON:	Finely thou'dst rule, alone, a land dispeopled!
CREON:	It seems this boy will plead the woman's cause.
HAEMON:	Woman art thou? my care is all for thee.
CREON:	Shameless—is't right to wrangle with thy father?
HAEMON:	I see that wrong for right thou dost mistake.
CREON:	Do I mistake, to reverence my office?
HAEMON:	What reverence, heaven's honours to contemn?
CREON:	O hateful spirit, ruled by a woman's will!
HAEMON:	To no base service shalt thou prove me bound.
CREON:	Art thou not pleading all the time for her?
HAEMON:	For thee and me, and for the gods below.
CREON:	Thou shalt not marry her, this side the grave.
HAEMON:	If she must die, she shall: but not alone.
CREON:	Art grown so bold, thou dost fly out in threats?
HAEMON:	What threats, to argue with a foolish purpose?
CREON:	Thou'lt rue—unwise—thy wisdom spent on me.
HAEMON:	Thou art my father; or wise I scarce had called thee.
CREON:	Slave—to thy mistress babble, not to me.
HAEMON:	Wouldst thou have all the talking for thine own?

CREON: Is't come to this? But, by Olympus yonder,
         Know well, thou shalt be sorry for these taunts,
         Wherewith thou dost upbraid me. Slaves, what ho!
         Bring that abhorrence hither, that she may die,
         Now, in her bridegroom's sight, whilst here he stands.

HAEMON: Neither in my sight—imagine no such thing—
         Shall she be slain; nor shalt thou from this hour
         Look with thine eyes upon my face again:
         To friends who love thy madness I commit thee.

         (*Exit Haemon.*)

CHORUS: Suddenly, sire, in anger he is gone:
         Young minds grow desperate, by grief distemper'd.

CREON: More than a man let him conceive and do;
         He shall not save these maidens from their doom.

CHORUS: Both sisters art thou purposed to destroy?

CREON: Not her whose hands sinned not; thou askest well.

CHORUS: What of the other? how shall she be slain?

CREON: By paths untrodden of men I will conduct her,
         And shut her, living in a vault, rock-hewn,
         And there, with food, no more than shall suffice
         To avert the guilt of murder from the city,
         To Hades, the one god whom she reveres,
         She, praying not to die, either shall have
         Her asking, or shall learn, albeit too late,
         That to revere the dead is fruitless toil.

         (*Exit Creon.*)

Strophe

CHORUS: O Love, our conqueror, matchless in might,
Thou prevailest, O Love, thou dividest the prey:
In damask cheeks of a maiden
Thy watch through the night is set.
Thou roamest over the sea;
On the hills, in the shepherds' huts, thou art;
Nor of deathless gods, nor of short-lived men,
From thy madness any escapeth.

Antistrophe

Unjust, through thee, are the thoughts of the just,
Thou dost bend them, O Love, to thy will, to thy spite.
Unkindly strife thou hast kindled,
This wrangling of son with sire.
For great laws, throned in the heart,
To the sway of a rival power give place,
To the love-light flashed from a fair bride's eyes:
In her triumph laughs Aphrodite.
Me, even now, me also,
Seeing these things, a sudden pity
Beyond all governance transports:
The fountains of my tears
I can refrain no more,
Seeing Antigone here to the bridal chamber
Come, to the all-receiving chamber of Death.

(Antigone is led out of the palace by guards.)

ANTIGONE: Friends and my countrymen, ye see me
Upon the last of all my ways
Set forth, the Sun-god's latest light
Beholding, now and never more:

But Death, who giveth sleep to all,
Yet living leads me hence
To the Acherontian shore,
Of marriage rites amerced,
And me no bridal song hath ever sung,
But Acheron will make of me his bride.

CHORUS: Therefore renowned, with praise of men,
To yonder vault o' the dead thou goest,
By no slow-wasting sickness stricken,
Nor doomed to fall with those who win
The wages of the swords they drew,
But, being to thyself a law,
Alone of mortals the dark road
To deathward, living, thou shalt tread.

ANTIGONE: I heard of one, most piteous in her ending,
That stranger, child of Phrygian Tantalus,
On heights of Sipylus enclasped,
And ivy-like enchained,
By clinging tendrils of the branching rock,
Who day and night unceasingly
'Mid drizzle of rain and drift of snow
Slow-wasting in her place
Stands, as the tale is told,
Her lids surcharged with weeping, and her neck
And bosom drenched with falling of her tears:—
A fate most like to hers
Seals up with sleep these eyes of mine.

CHORUS: She was a goddess, sprung from gods:
Mortals, of mortal birth, are we.
But for one dead to win with those
Who rank no lower than the gods—
In life and afterwards in death—
An equal lot, were much to hear.

ANTIGONE: Ah, I am mocked! Nay, by our fathers' gods,
Withhold thy taunts till I am gone—
Gone and evanished from thy sight.
O Thebes, my city!
O wealthy men of Thebes!
But *ye* will witness—yes, to you I turn—
O fount Dircaean, and this sacred grove
O Thebè the fair-charioted,
By what stern law, and how of friends unwept,
To that strange grave I go,
The massy dungeon for my burial heaped.
O luckless wight,
Exiled from earth nor housed below,
Both by the living and the dead disowned!

CHORUS: To furthest brink of boldness thou didst stray,
And stumbling there, at foot of Justice' throne,
Full heavily, my daughter, hast thou fallen:
Yet of thy father's fault belike
This suffering pays the price.

ANTIGONE: Thou hast touched, ev'n there, my bitterest pang of all,
A thrice-told tale, my father's grief—
And all our grievous doom that clung
About the famed Labdacidae.
O that incestuous bed
Of horror, and my father's sin—
The hapless mother who bore him to the light,
By him enclasped—wherefrom I luckless sprang:
With whom, accurst, unwedded,
I must go hence to dwell.
O brother, a bride ill-starred
Who to thy couch didst win,
How, being dead, me living thou hast slain!

CHORUS: Religion prompts the reverent deed:

171

But power, to whomso power belongs,
Must nowise be transgressed; and thee
A self-willed temper hath o'erthrown.

ANTIGONE: Unwept and unfriended,
Cheered by no song Hymenaeal—
Lo, I am led, heavy-hearted,
This road that awaits me.
The sacred light-giving eye in heaven
Now no more must I see, unhappy:
But for my fate not a tear falls,
Not a friend makes moan.

(Enter Creon.)

CREON: Know ye not, songs and weepings before death
That none would pretermit, were he allowed?
Hence with her, hence, and tarry not, but deep
In her tomb-prison, even as I have said,
Leave her alone, forsaken: to die, or else
Live, in that vault entombed, if so she will:
Since of this maiden's blood our hands are clean,
Only we ban her sojourn in the light.

ANTIGONE: O tomb! O nuptial chamber! O house deep-delved
In earth, safe-guarded ever! To thee I come,
And to my kin in thee, who many an one
Are with Persephone, dead among the dead:
And last of all, most miserably by far,
I thither am going, ere my life's term be done.
But a good hope I cherish, that, come there,
My father's love will greet me, yea and thine,
My mother—and thy welcome, brother dear:
Since, when ye died, I with mine own hands laved
And dressed your limbs, and poured upon your graves

Libations; and like service done to thee
Hath brought me, Polyneices, now to this.
Yet well I honoured thee, the wise will say:
Since not for children's sake would I, their mother,
Nor for my husband, slain, and mouldering there,
Have travailed thus, doing despite to Thebes.
According to what law, do I speak this?
One husband slain, another might have been,
And children from another, losing these;
But, father and mother buried out of sight,
There can be born no brother any more.
Such was the law whereby I held thee first
In honour; but to Creon all mistaken,
O dear my brother, I seemed, and overbold—
And now, made captive thus, he leads me hence
No wife, no bride for ever—of marriage-joy
And nursery of children quite bereft:
So by my friends forsaken I depart,
Living, unhappy, to dim vaults of death.
Yet I transgressed—what ordinance of heaven?
Why to the gods, ill-fated, any more
Should I look up—whom call to succour—since
Impiety my piety is named?
But, if these things are pleasing to the gods,
I'll freely own I suffered for my fault;
If theirs the fault, who doomed me, may to them
No worse befall than they unjustly do!

CHORUS: Stormily still o'er the soul of the maiden
           The selfsame gusts of passion sweep.

CREON: Therefore, I warn them, ruth for their lingering,
           To those who lead her, this shall cause.

ANTIGONE: Short shrift, swift death—ah! woe is me—
           This speech portends.

CREON: Lay to thy soul no flattering hope,
That unfulfilled this doom may be.

ANTIGONE: O country of Thebes and my father's city,
And gods my progenitors,
Lo, how they lead me—now, and delay not.
O all ye princes of Thebes, behold me—
Of the race of your kings, me, sole surviving—
What things at the hands of what men I suffer,
For the fear of the gods I feared.

(*Exit Antigone.*)

Strophe 1

CHORUS: Out of the sunlight so,
In brass-bound prison-courts,
Were pent the limbs of Danaë,
And in a living tomb sealed up from sight;
Albeit, O daughter, she as thou
Came of a noble line,
And that life-quickening treasure of his golden rain
She had in charge from Zeus to keep.
O dread mysterious power of fate,
That neither wealth nor war can quell,
Nor walls shut out, nor ships escape,
Dark-fleeing o'er the foam!

Antistrophe 1

And that Edonian king
Was bound, the choleric son
Of Dryas, splenetive and hot,
Fast in the rock by Dionysus chained.
Such fierce and fevered issue streams

174

From madness at the height.
With splenetive rash speech what madness had assailed
The vengeful god, too late he learned.
To women-worshippers inspired
Their torchlit revels he forbade,
And flutings that the Muses loved
Had silenced with his scorn.

Strophe 2

From the dark rock-portals of the divided sea
Here go the cliffs of Bosporus, and there
The savage Thracian coast
Of Salmydessus, where the neighbour-worshipped God
Of Battle saw the blinding blow accurst,
Dealt by that fierce stepdame,
Darkling descend on both the sons
Of Phineus—on their sightless orbs
That plead for vengeance, stricken through and stabbed
By the sharp shuttle in her murderous hands.

Antistrophe 2

Wasted with their sorrow, their mother's hapless fate
They hapless wept, and in their mother's shame
Had part, as those base-born:
Yet she from the old Erechtheid blood her birth derived,
And in deep caverns of the hills was nursed,
Amid her father's storms,
Child of the North-wind—up the steep
Hillsides no bounding foal so fleet,
A daughter of the gods: but her, O child,
Fate's everlasting hands availed to reach.

(Enter Teiresias, led by a boy.)

TEIRESIAS: Prince of Thebes, we come—one sight for both
Our common road descrying, as behoves
Blind men to find their way by help of others.

CREON: What tidings, old Teiresias, dost thou bring?

TEIRESIAS: Hear then the prophet, and attend his speech.

CREON: Have I aforetime from thy wisdom swerved?

TEIRESIAS: So, clear of shoals, thou pilotest the state.

CREON: The service thou hast rendered I attest.

TEIRESIAS: Once more on razor's edge thy fortunes stand.

CREON: Hearing thy speech, I shudder: tell me more.

TEIRESIAS: My art's prognostications hear and judge.
For in my ancient seat, to watch the birds
In that their general gathering-place, I sat,
And heard an unintelligible noise,
A cry and clangour of birds, confused with rage;
And what fierce fray they waged with murderous claws,
I guessed too surely by the whirr of wings.
Scared by that sound, burnt-offerings I then
Essayed on blazing altars; but no flame
Leapt from the sacrifice; a clammy ooze
Reeked from the thighs, and 'mid the ashes dripped,
Smoking and sputtering; the gall disparted,
And on the air was spent; and the thigh-bones
Of the enfolding fat fell stripped and bare.
This from this boy I heard, whose eyes beheld
The failing signs of sacrifice obscure:
Others by me are guided, I by him.
And by thy will we are afflicted thus.
For now our hearths and altars everyone

Have ravening dogs and birds fouled with the flesh
Of this poor fallen son of Oedipus;
And so no flame of victims burnt may move
Gods any more to hearken to our prayers,
And birds obscence flap forth a bodeful cry,
With fat of human carrion newly gorged.
Slight not, my son, such warning. For all men,
Both great and small, are liable to err:
But he who errs no more unfortunate
Or all unwise shall be, if having tripped
He rights the wrong nor stubbornly persists.
He who persists in folly is the fool.
Give death his due: stab not the fallen foe:
What valour is in this, to slay the slain?
Wisely I speak and well; and sweet it is
To hear good counsel, when it counsels gain.

CREON: Old man, ye all, as bowmen at a mark,
Shoot at this man, and with your prophecies
Ye practise on me too, and mine own kin
Mere merchandise and salework make of me.
Go to, get gain, and barter, if ye will,
Amber ye buy from Sardis, and fine gold
Of Ind: but him, I say, ye shall not bury:
No, not if eagles, ministers of Zeus,
Should bear him piecemeal to their Master's throne,
Will I, for fear of such pollution, grant
Leave for his burial; knowing well that men
Soil not the stainless majesty of heaven.
But, aged seer, the wisest of mankind
Dishonourably may fall, who fairly speak
Dishonourable words, and all for gain.

TEIRESIAS: Alas!
Who knows, or who considers, in this world—

CREON: What wilt thou say? What commonplace is this?

TEIRESIAS: How prudence is the best of all our wealth?

CREON: As folly, I suppose, our deadliest hurt.

TEIRESIAS: Yet with this malady art thou possest.

CREON: Reproaches I'll not bandy with the prophet.

TEIRESIAS: Saying that I falsely prophesy, thou dost.

CREON: So are all prophets; 'tis a covetous race.

TEIRESIAS: Greed of base gain marks still the tyrant-sort.

CREON: Knowest thou that of thy rulers this is said?

TEIRESIAS: I know; for thou through me didst save the state.

CREON: Wise in thy craft art thou, but false at heart.

TEIRESIAS: Secrets, fast-locked, thou'lt move me to disclose.

CREON: Unlock them, only speaking not for gain.

TEIRESIAS: So, for thy part indeed, methinks I shall.

CREON: Think not that in my purpose thou shalt trade.

TEIRESIAS: But surely know that thou not many more
Revolving courses of the sun shalt pass,
Ere of thine own blood one, to make amends,
Dead for the dead, thou shalt have rendered up,
For that a living soul thou hast sent below,
And with dishonour in the grave hast lodged,
And that one dead thou holdest here cut off
From presence of the gods who reign below,
All rites of death, all obsequies denied—
With whom thou shouldst not meddle, nor the gods
In heaven, but of their due thou robb'st the dead.

Therefore of Hades and the gods for thee
The Avengers wait, with ruin slow yet sure,
To take thee in the pit which thou hast dug.
Do I speak this for gold? Thyself shalt judge:
For, yet a little while, and wailings loud
Of men and women in thy house shall show.
Think, of each city too what gathering rage,
That sees its mangled dead entombed in maws
Of dogs and all fierce beasts, or borne by kites
With stench unhallowed to its hearth-crowned heights.
So like a bowman have I launched at thee
In wrath, for thou provok'st me, shafts indeed
To pierce thy heart, and fail not, from whose smart
Thou'lt not escape. But now, boy, lead me home,
That he may vent his spleen on younger men,
And learn to keep a tongue more temperate,
And in his breast a better mind than now.

(*Exit Teiresias.*)

CHORUS: The man has prophesied dread things, O King,
And gone: and never have I known—not since
These temples changed their raven locks to snow—
That aught of false this city heard from him.

CREON: Yea, this I know, and much am I perplexed:
For hard it is to yield, but standing firm
I fear to pluck swift ruin on my pride.

CHORUS: Son of Menoeceus, be advised in time.

CREON: Say then, what must I do? and I'll obey.

CHORUS: Go, from her prison in the rock release
The maiden, and the unburied corpse inter.

CREON: Dost thou think this, and wouldst thou have me yield?

CHORUS: Yea, King, and quickly; for the gods cut short
With sudden scathe the foolishness of men.

CREON: Hardly indeed, but yet with forced consent
I'll do it, stooping to necessity.

CHORUS: Do it, and go; leave not this task to others.

CREON: Even as I am, I'll go; and, servants, haste,
That hear and hear me not: axes in hand,
All to yon spot, far-seen, make good your speed.
But I, since this way now my mind is bent,
Whom I myself have bound, myself will loose.
For now my heart misgives me, he lives best,
Whose feet depart not from the ancient ways.

(*Exit Creon.*)

Strophe 1

CHORUS: Worshipped by many names—
Glory of Theban Semele,
Child of loud-thundering Zeus—
Haunting the famed Italian fields
Whom as a prince the hospitable vale
Of the Eleusinian Dame reveres—
Bacchus, that hast thy home
In Thebes, the home of Bacchanals,
Beside Ismenus' fertile stream,
Where the fell dragon's teeth of old were sown.

Antistrophe 1

O'er the two-crested peak,
With nymphs Corycian in thy train,
By springs of Castaly,

The streaming levin lights thy path:
And from steep Nysa's hills, with ivy clad,
And that green slope, with clustering grapes
Empurpled to the sea,
When thou wouldst visit Theban streets,
A jocund company divine
With acclamation loud conducts thee forth.

Strophe 2

Thebes of all cities most thou honourest,
Thou with thy mother, whom the lightning slew:
And now, when Thebes is sick,
And all her people the sore plague hath stricken,
Hear us and come with healing feet
O'er the Parnassian hill,
Or the resounding strait.

Antistrophe 2

Come, whom fire-breathing stars in dance obey,
The master of the voices of the night,
Of Zeus the puissant son—
Come at our call, girt with thy Thyiad troop,
That follow, with thy frenzy filled,
Dancing the livelong night,
Iacchus, thee their lord.

(*Enter a Messenger.*)

MESSENGER: Neighbours of Cadmus, and the royal house
Of old Amphion, no man's life would I,
How high or low soever, praise or blame,
Since, who to-day has fortune, good or ill,

To-morrow's fortune lifts or lays him low;
No seer a constant lot foresees for men.
For Creon before was happy, as I deemed,
Who saved this land of Cadmus from its foes,
And the sole sovereignty of Thebes receiving
Prospered therein, with noble children blest.
Now all is lost. For, when the joys of life
Men have relinquished, no more life indeed
I count their living, but a living death.
For in thy house heap riches, if thou wilt;
Keep kingly state; yet, if no joy withal
Thou hast, for all things else, compared with pleasure,
I would not change the shadow of a smoke.

CHORUS: Of what grief now of princes wilt thou tell?

MESSENGER: That one lies dead, whom those who live have slain.

CHORUS: Say, who is slain? And what man is the slayer?

MESSENGER: Haemon is dead: his death no stranger's act.

CHORUS: Slain by himself, or by his father's hand?

MESSENGER: Wroth with his pitiless sire, he slew himself.

CHORUS: O prophet, how thy prophecy comes true!

MESSENGER: These things being so, consider of the rest.

CHORUS: Lo, hard at hand the miserable Queen,
Eurydice: who from the house comes forth
Either by chance, or hearing of her son.

(*Enter Eurydice.*)

EURYDICE: Good townsmen all, your conference I heard,
As to the doors I came, intending now
Of Pallas to entreat her heavenly aid.

Even as I loosed the fastenings of the gate,
That opened wide, there smote my ears a word
Of sorrow all my own: backward I swooned,
Surprised by terror, in my maidens' arms:
But tell me now your tidings once again—
For, not unlearned in sorrow, I shall hear.

MESSENGER: Dear mistress, I will tell thee what I saw,
And not leave out one word of all the truth.
Why should I flatter thee with glozing words,
Too soon found false? Plain truth is ever best.
Thy husband hence I followed at the heels
To that high plain, where torn by dogs the body
Of Polyneices lay, unpitied still.
A prayer we said to Hecate in the way
And Pluto, their displeasure to refrain,
Then, sprinkling with pure water, in new-stript boughs
Wrapped round and burned the fragments that re-
    mained.
A lofty funeral-mound of native earth
We heaped for him; then sought the maiden's bed,
Her bridal bed with Hades in the rock.
And from afar a voice of shrill lament
About the unhallowed chamber someone heard,
And came to Creon, and told it to his lord.
And in his ears, approaching, the wild cry
Rang doubtfully, till now there brake for him
A word of sharp despair, "O wretched man,
What fear is at my heart? and am I going
The wofullest road that ever I have gone?
It is my son's voice greets me. Good servants, go,
Go nearer quickly; and standing by the tomb,
Even to the throat of the vault peer through and look,
Where the wrenched stonework gapes, if Haemon's voice
I recognise indeed, or by the gods

Am cheated!" Crazed with his fear, he spake; and we
Looked, as he bade; and in the last of the tomb
We saw the maiden—hanged: about her neck
Some shred of linen had served her for a noose:
And fallen upon her, clasping her, he lay,
Wailing his wasted passion in the grave,
His fatal father, and his luckless bride.
His father saw, and crying a bitter cry
Went in, and with a lamentable voice
Called him, "O rash, what is it that thou hast done?
What wouldst thou? On what madness hast thou rushed?
My son, come forth: I pray thee—I implore."
But with fierce eyes the boy glared at his sire
And looks of loathing, and for answer plucked
Forth a two-hilted sword, and would have struck,
But missed him, as he fled: and in that minute,
Wroth with himself, in his own side amain
Thrust deep the steel, unhappy; and conscious still
Folded the maiden in his fainting arms;
Then, gasping out his life in one sharp breath,
Pelted her pale cheek with the crimson shower.
Dead with the dead he lies, such nuptial rites
In halls of Hades, luckless, having won;
Teaching the world, that of all human ills
With human folly is none that may compare.

(*Exit Eurydice.*)

CHORUS: How should one deem of this? The Queen, without
            A word, of good or evil, has gone hence.

MESSENGER: Indeed, 'tis strange: but yet I feed on hope
            That to lament in public for her son
            She will not deign; but, as for private sorrow,

> Will charge her women in the house to weep.
> She is well tried in prudence, not to fail.

CHORUS:
> I know not; but to me the too-much silence,
> No less than clamorous grief, seems perilous.

MESSENGER:
> I will go hence to the house, and know, if aught
> Of secret purpose in her raging heart
> She hath kept locked from us. Thou sayest well:
> The too-much silence may bode mischief too.

(Exit the Messenger.)

CHORUS:
> Lo, the King comes hither himself, in his hands
> The record, not doubtful its purport, bearing;
> No grief (I dare to say) wrought by another,
> But the weight of his own misdoing.

(Enter Creon with the body of Haemon.)

Strophe

CREON:
> Alas, my purblind wisdom's fatal fault,
> Stubborn, and fraught with death!
> Ye see us, sire and son,
> The slayer and the slain.
> O counsels all unblest!
> Alas for thee, my son,
> So young a life and so untimely quenched—
> Gone from me, past recall—
> Not by thy folly, but my own!

CHORUS:
> Ah, how too late thou dost discern the truth!

CREON:
> Yea, to my cost I know: but then, methinks,
> Oh then, some god with crushing weight

185

Leapt on me, drave me into frantic ways,
Trampling, alas for me,
In the base dust my ruined joy.
O toil and trouble of mortals—trouble and toil!

(*Enter a Second Messenger.*)

SECOND
MESSENGER:
Trouble, O King, thine own and none but thine,
Thou comest, methinks, part bearing in thy hands;
Part—in the house thou hast, and soon shalt see.

CREON: What more, what worse than evil, yet remains?

SECOND
MESSENGER:
Thy wife is dead, with desperate hand ev'n now
Self-slain, for this dead son for whom she lived.

Antistrophe

CREON:
O harbour of Hades, never to be appeased,
Why art thou merciless?
What heavy news is this?
Harsh news to me of grief,
That slays me, slain before!
A woful word indeed,
Telling of slaughter upon slaughter heaped,
To me, the twice-bereaved,
At one fell swoop, of son and wife!

CHORUS: Behold and see: for now the doors stand wide.

CREON:
This second grief, ah me, my eyes behold.
What fate, ah what, remains behind?
My son I hold already in my arms:
And now, ah woe is me,
This other in my sight lies dead:
Mother and child—most piteous both to see!

SECOND MESSENGER:	Heartstricken at the altar as she fell, Her swooning eyes she opened, and made moan For Megareus, her son, who nobly died Before, and for this other, and with her last Breath cursed, the slayer of her children, thee.
CREON:	Ah me, will no one aim Against my heart, made wild with fear. With two-edged sword a deadly thrust? O wretched that I am, Fulfilled with sorrow, and made one with grief!
SECOND MESSENGER:	She did reproach thee, truly, ere she died And laid on thee the blame of both their deaths.
CREON:	What was the manner of her violent end?
SECOND MESSENGER:	Pierced to the heart, by her own hand, she died, Hearing her son's most lamentable fate.
CREON:	All, all on me this guilt must ever rest, And on no head but mine. O my poor son, I slew thee, even I: Let no one doubt, but that the deed was mine. O servants, lead me quickly, lead me hence; And let me be as one who is no more.
CHORUS:	'Tis counselled well, if well with ill can be: For bad is best, when soonest out of sight.
CREON:	I care not, let it come: Let come the best of all my fate, The best, the last, that ends my days: What care I? come what will— That I no more may see another day.
CHORUS:	Let be the future: mind the present need, And leave the rest to whom the rest concerns.

CREON: No other wish have I; that prayer is all.

CHORUS: Pray not at all: all is as fate appoints:
           'Tis not in mortals to avert their doom.

CREON: Oh lead me hence, unprofitable; who thee
           Unwittingly have slain,
           Child, and my wife, unhappy; and know not now
           Which way to look to either: for all things
           Are crooked that I handle, and a fate
           Intolerable upon my life hath leapt.

           (*Creon is led away.*)

CHORUS: First of all happiness far is wisdom,
           And to the gods that one fail not of piety.
           But great words of the overweening
           Lay great stripes to the backs of the boasters:
           Taught by adversity,
           Old age learns, too late, to be wise.